History
of the
Industrial Revolution
in
Western Maryland

Patrick H. Stakem

Copyright © 2010, 2014

2nd Edition
Number 3 in the Western Maryland Series

"Whoever wishes to foresee the future must consult the
past…"
Niccolo Machiavelli, 1513

"Men have become the tools of their tools."
Henry David Thoreau

Table of Contents

Author

The author grew up in Cumberland, MD, across the street from the location of Fort Cumberland.

Mr. Stakem is a member of the Council of the Alleghenies, as well as the Western Maryland Chapter of the National Railway Historical Society, the Mount Savage Historical Society, the Westernport Heritage Society, and the C&O Canal Association. He currently resides in Laurel, MD. He has published numerous articles and books on the railroads, canal, and industrial and transportation heritage of Western Maryland. He is associated with Loyola University in Maryland and the Johns Hopkins University.

Introduction

The Nineteenth Century saw a period of rapid technology development, as steam power was applied to many aspects of manufacturing and transportation. People's lives became better, old things could be done more cheaply or faster, and new things were enabled. At the same time, machinery displaced jobs and switched the economy from a focus on agriculture to a new focus on manufacturing. A new age was being born, and birth involves pain, disruption, and change. The discovery of copious amounts of coal near Eckhart was in 1814, with the production of iron in Lonaconing beginning in 1839.

Generally, we speak of the first Industrial Revolution wrapping up in the middle of the 19th Century, and the 2nd Industrial Revolution, which built upon the first, continuing into the 20th Century. The second Industrial Revolution, building upon the products of the first, kicked off a period of rapid industrialization. With advances in energy, manufacturing, and production. The products of the 1st Including iron, drove the products of the 2nd, locomotives and such. This we see in Mount Savage.

Steam technology relied on the extractive industries for coal, iron ore, and other materials. There was a seemingly limitless demand for the raw materials and finished products of the steam age. A huge number of jobs were created, and fewer farmers were needed to feed the population. Vast patterns of migration brought Europeans to the America to share the Dream.

Britain was the first to go through the disruption of the Industrial Revolution, and British Technology was the model for the United States. The U.S. looked to Britain for "lessons learned" on canal, railroad, and factory technology. All over the country, enclaves of technology sprang up, centered around the abundance of raw materials, or the availability of cheap power and transportation, enabled by streams and rivers.

The elements required for a successful technology venture in the Industrial Revolution were: raw materials, labor, capital, technological expertise, and transportation. The cost of transportation touches all the other aspects. In

England, a good canal network allowed raw materials to be shipped for processing, or product such as pig iron to be shipped to users from an area where the material was abundant. Capital began to accumulate when manufacturing of goods on a large scale became possible. Capitalism, with wages, attracted large numbers of laborers to factory's and mines. Finally, a small cadre of engineers and practitioners made continuous improvements in processes and machinery. A master ironsmith was worth his weight in gold, because he could apply the processes and co-ordinate the labor to produce the desired products. Wales became the major supplier of iron making expertise. England became the major supplier of Capital. Europe became the major supplier of cheap labor.

In New England, the Manufacturing centers such as Lowell in Massachusetts were built near streams. Facilities in New York used water powered hammers and blowing engines to produce machine parts from iron ore. The technology fed on itself. These machines were shipped by ocean-going sailing ships, shallow draft riverboats, and canal boats to remote locations where raw materials were plentiful. The Industrial Revolution pulled itself up by its own bootstraps – It enabled the cheaper transportation and more widespread distribution of not only capital goods, but also the means to produce capital goods.

The earliest industrial activities in Maryland occurred in the East, near the coast . In colonial times, raw materials were exported to England. For example, Maryland exported pig iron. After Independence, the States controlled the manufacturing ventures, providing them with charters, the right to exclusive use of a stream of water, and the right to build roads across others' property. The main motive power of the engines of commerce was water, and charcoal was the main fuel. Massive amounts of trees were cut to keep the furnaces going. Since the finished product, pigs of iron, were heavy, the need for proximity to water transportation was obvious. The industry's developed where the raw materials were in close proximity to port facility's. In the Western end of the State, vast beds of coal and iron lay waiting to be exploited. The iron furnace facility at Lonaconing used coke (derived from coal), not charcoal (derived from wood) as an advance in technology. But Lonaconing suffered from a transportation problem, which would not be solved until too late to matter. The coke furnace technology made its way to Mount Savage, where the juxtaposition of coal, iron ore, limestone, and fire clay defined the obvious spot for a technology enclave. The transportation problem was solved by a railroad, using rails built on site. The rail line ran to Cumberland, where the Baltimore & Ohio Railroad provided transportation to the Port of Baltimore, and the Chesapeake & Ohio Canal was coming to provide cheap transportation to the manufacturing center of Georgetown and the Port of Alexandria.

This was all enabled by many factors in conjunction: the availability of raw materials, of which the US had vast, untouched sources; the availability of cheap labor, of which the United States also had a seemingly limitless supply, and Capital. The latter came from far-sighted Captains of Industry, later to be viewed as greedy robber barons, who had accumulated enough money to make things happen. The banking industry was in its infancy, and these speculative ventures were funded by wealthy individuals and families.

The financing and impetus for the early ventures was not provided by Government, but by entrepreneurial individuals coming together with a profit motive. It can be argued that the collapse of the Mount Savage iron operation was directly related to the Government tariff on imported iron – an international trade issue.

In terms of Transportation Infrastructure, the National Road Project was a Federally funded project, with maintenance left to the States. Both the Baltimore & Ohio Railroad and the Chesapeake & Ohio Canal Projects were accomplished by Corporations, albeit with quite a few shares owned by Federal, States, and Municipal Governments. Creative financing for the Canal developed a new approach, Preferred stock.

Revolution brings change, and change is both bad and good. The old proven ways are superseded by new ways of doing things. People's lives are changed. Society refocuses on new goals. A lot is lost by the wayside.

Maryland was no different than the rest of the country or the world, and provided a microcosm of what was happening at large. Maryland ranges from seaports with access to the Atlantic via the Chesapeake Bay on the east, to mountains at the west. Travel less than 100 miles west from the bay, and the terrain changes drastically, to the north-south running Appalachians, which present a barrier to traffic. The Port of Baltimore was in competition with Philadelphia, New York, and other port city's along the Atlantic seaboard to connect with the rest of the country past the Appalachians, which had a vast network of navigable north-south water routes, the Ohio leading to the Mississippi. In the early 19th century, canals were being pushed westward, and the possibility of railroads was being explored. President Jefferson kicked off a program of "internal improvement" when the Federally funded National Road headed west from Cumberland in 1811. The B&O Railroad started building toward the Ohio River in 1828. On the very same day, the Chesapeake and Ohio Canal started westward from the industrial enclave and port at Georgetown. The importance of transportation was recognized by the Federal Government, the States, and entrepreneurs.

Let us focus in on Maryland, specifically, western Maryland. A gap in the Appalachian range was found at the confluence of Will's Creek and the Potomac. This was known since George Washington surveyed the territory in the early 1700's. The National Road, the canal, and the railroad headed toward that gap. The western end of Maryland had vast resources of coal, some of which were discovered when construction workers for the National Road broke through a huge seam of coal (the "Big Vein") in Eckhart, just east of Frostburg. The rest of the country was hungry for coal. A lot of the big cities had exhausted their supply of nearby trees. The factories of the industrial revolution demanded more and more fuel in addition to that needed for cooking and heating houses. The Baltimore & Ohio Railroad evaluated Big Vein coal, which had been brought to Baltimore by wagon, and the Federal Arsenal at Harper's Ferry received coal by flat-bottomed riverboats.

And then things started to happen quickly. At Mount Savage, some 10 miles west of Cumberland, vast reserves of iron ore were discovered. Mount Savage was close to the coal mines, and close to huge outcroppings of limestone. And, of all things, refractory-grade clay was found. That is all the industrial revolution required, besides some money and some cheap labor. The cheap labor came from Wales and Ireland and all over Europe. The money came from England and New York.

This book explores three specific 19th century industrial sites in Allegany County, in the west of Maryland. These include the iron furnace facility at the village of Lonaconing, the coal from Eckhart Mines, and the integrated industrial research, development, and production facility at Mount Savage, which wound up producing entire locomotives for export sale, and was at one time the largest producer of iron in the nation.

The time frame covered spans from the early part of the 19th century, although not much was happening until the 1840's or so, until the end of the century. Most of the interesting projects were in place and completed before the Civil War years. After that, it was a continuation of some industry's, and the building up of new ones. Generally, the Industrial Revolution in the United States was going until 1840, 1866 at a stretch. After that, the second Industrial Revolution built upon the first, and was running until the 1870's

There were other industrial revolution projects going on, that we will not focus on here. Cumberland had an iron furnace, and later, extensive steel works. A tin-plating mill was successful for many years, and there was a large glass industry. Major railroad shops continue working to this day in south Cumberland. Steam cars were manufactured in Luke, Maryland, on the border with West Virginia. The boatyards for the C&O Canal were located at Cumberland. There was a steam powered sawmill in the Green Ridge Forest. The Bowery Iron Furnace was located south of Frostburg at Midlothian. All these are topics for future exploration. This second edition has been updated, reorganized, and corrected, with new material and references.

Author

Mr. Stakem is the Historian, Western Maryland Chapter, National Railway Historical Society, Cumberland, MD, and a member of the Mt. Savage Historical Society, Council of the Alleghenies, Preservation Society of Allegany County (MD), C&O Canal Historical Society, Mountain State Railroad & Logging Historical Association (WV), Railway & Locomotive

Historical Society, Inc., Western Maryland Railway Historical Society (Union Bridge, MD). He is from Cumberland, Md.

Eckhart Mines

Located near Frostburg on either side of the National Road, the sleepy village of Eckhart Mines was once a bustling industrial center of mining and railroad activity. Coal was discovered in Eckhart around 1814, during the construction of the National Road. This was convenient, as the coal could be moved to Cumberland by wagon, and floated down the Potomac River, when conditions permitted. The coal from Eckhart started the Maryland coal trade in 1843.

Eckhart Mines is an unincorporated town in Allegany County, Maryland. The population is around 150. Eckhart Mines lies at the southwestern base of Federal Hill, about 2 miles east of Frostburg and one mile northeast of Clarysville. It was originally founded as a company town. The Eckhart Mines' location up Braddock Run was among the first bituminous coal mines developed in the area, together with a few others within the Georges Creek Valley. The Eckhart operation was owned by the Maryland Mining Company.

Most of the predecessor mining companies had the name 'Iron' in their names. Both Lonaconing, in the Georges Creek region, and Mount Savage, had supplies of ore, and were involved in iron production. Only Eckhart never developed its iron deposits. However, by 1842 coal quickly became the cargo of choice for the railroads. The eastern industrial centers of Baltimore and Georgetown needed fuel for their furnaces. Large cities such as Baltimore had depleted the easily accessible supplies of firewood for home heating and industry. Coal, once overlooked, was becoming the lifeblood of the cities, industry, and the railroads. The need for coal as a substitute for firewood, its value to industry as a fuel, and the ability to move enough of it from the mines to the users all developed together. In addition, the technology for using the hotter burning coal for home heating and industry was developed.

Eckhart was originally settled as military lots 3681 and 3682, granted to Jacob Loar and his brother Abraham for their service in the Revolution. Jacob's wife was Sarah Eckhart, daughter of George Adam Eckhart (variously spelled Eckart, Eckert, or Eckhart). Jacob was born in Rotterdam, and had been a Private in the 3rd company, 7th Battalion of the York (Pennsylvania) Militia in 1785.

George Adam Eckhart was born in 1729 in Bavaria, and died in 1806 in Eckhart Mines. He married Anna M. Wittmeyer in 1755. She was born in Germany.

George Eckhart sailed from Rotterdam, Holland on the ship *Union*, the same ship as Jacob Loar. He settled some 10 miles west of Cumberland in the year 1780. A small village sprung up on George's land, which was named Eckhart Mines and is said to have been named for him. The village was laid out July 12, 1789. George and Mary Eckhart had 5 children, one of whom was Sarah. Not much exciting happened there until the construction of the National Road cut through the upper end of the "Big Vein" of coal, which extends down the Georges Creek Valley, and provided hundreds of millions of tons of product during its operation.

Companies
This section discusses the companies involved in the building of Eckhart Mines as a town to support the mining and railroad industries.

<u>Maryland Mining Company</u>

The Maryland Mining Company (MMC) was incorporated in Maryland on March 12, 1829. The incorporators were Nicholas G. Ridgeley, Hugh McElderry, Brice W. Howard, Samuel Keerle, George McCulloch, William McMahon, George Brown, Hugh W. Evans, and John Thomas.

Nicholas G. Ridgeley (1771-1829) was a grocery merchant in Baltimore. His grandson, also Nicholas G., was born in 1834, became a doctor, and served in the Civil War It is unclear which of these was associated with the Company.

Hugh McElderry was a prominent merchant in Baltimore, and served as Director of the Baltimore & Ohio Railroad in 1829-1830, representing the interests of the City of Baltimore. He served on the Senate Finance Committee in 1834, and was a "secret partner" in the Bank of Maryland.

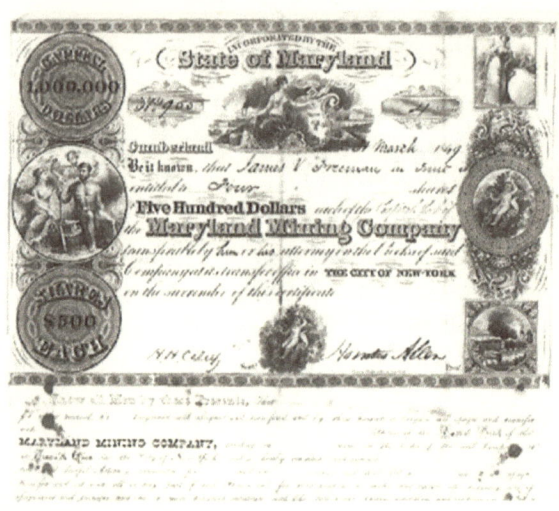

Brice W. Howard of Allegany County is mentioned in conjunction with the 1823 Act of the Maryland Assembly to incorporate the Maryland Hospital. He is not referred to as a Doctor.

Samuel Keerle was from Baltimore, and served as a Director of the Fireman's Insurance Company. He may have been associated with the First Baltimore Bank.

George McCulloch (1792-1861) was a Democratic member of the House of Representatives from Pennsylvania. He was an ironmaster, and a proprietor of the Hannah Furnace (1830-1850) west of Johnstown, PA.

William McMahon served in the Maryland House of Delegates as a representative for Allegany County in 1808.

George Brown (1787-1859) was an Irish-American investment banker with an interest in railroads. He immigrated to Baltimore in 1802. His father was Alexander Brown, of the firm Alex. Brown & Sons, one of the leading investment banks in the United States in the 19th century. A meeting hosted at

George Brown's home in 1827 lead to the formation of the Baltimore & Ohio Railroad. At a subsequent meeting at his home, a committee studying the canal versus railroads issue concluded that Maryland would benefit more from railroads. He was an officer of the Mechanics Bank of Baltimore, which financed the sale of B&O stock for construction. He served as the first treasurer of the B&O, and succeeded his Father as head of Alex. Brown & Sons.

Hugh W. Evans was the President of Union Bank and a director of the Baltimore & Ohio Railroad.

John Chew Thomas (1764-1836) was a lawyer from Anne Arundel County, Maryland. He was elected as a Federalist to the Sixth congress, and served from 1799 to 1801. He declined to stand for re-election, and moved to Pennsylvania, where he resided until his death.

The Maryland Mining Company built the railroad from Eckhart to Will's Creek, a length of 9 miles, and later extended the line as the Potomac Wharf Branch. The original line was built by a company in which Henry R. Hazelhurst was a partner. Originally, Henry worked for the B&O Surveyor, Knight, drawing maps. He was a cousin and brother-in-law of Benjamin Latrobe. Henry surveyed several of the B&O lines. Later the B&O Corps of Engineers was "under the direction of H. R. Hazlehurst, Esq." The Cumberland *Alleganian* of August 30, 1845 reported that the Maryland Mining Company Railroad "was constructed by Gonder & Hazlehurst Co. who completed 9 ½ miles in 3 months." It was ¾ complete, with 2 tunnels remaining. The total rise was 1117 feet from Cumberland to Eckhart. Five miles were at 130 feet per miles (2.5%). The B&O's benchmark 17-Mile grade is 2.2%. The Eckhart Branch provided the B&O and the entire railroad industry with a not-to-exceed grade number. Luckily, the tonnage freight went downhill.

The company that delivered coal from the Maryland Mining Company to the B&O was Atkinson & Hazlehurst. They supplied coal to the B&O for testing in locomotives in 1838. It went by wagon on the National Road. The Allegany coal trade kicked off in December 1843 when coal went from Eckhart to

Cumberland by wagon on the National Road. There, it was loaded on the B&O to travel to dam #6 on the C&O canal west of Hancock, where it was transferred to canal boats for the trip to Georgetown. There, it was loaded on sailing ships for the journey to New York. And, New York was glad to get it.

Maryland Mining was to use "immense locomotives of 25 tons weight, of B&O design and constructed by James Murray." Mr. Murray was Superintendent of Motive Power for the B&O, and approved of Ross Winans' Camel engines, which were then being tested by the B&O for heavy haul.

Camel locomotive, author's collection

Maryland Mining Company was also authorized to operate a bank in Cumberland, the Mineral Bank. The Maryland Mining Company and its railroad were purchased by the Cumberland Coal & Iron Company in 1852.

The Maryland Mining Company Railway from Eckhart Mines to Will's Creek following Braddock Run was completed in 1846. Will's Creek was bridged at the west end of the Narrows with a four arch brick structure that stood until removed for flood control in 1998. The railway included two tunnels, the one closest to Cumberland (lower tunnel) being 506 feet in length, and the upper tunnel being 335 feet long. The tunnels were separated by 0.6 mile. The grade reached 3 percent in places. This branch was also the location of a large horseshoe curve at Clarysville. The construction of Interstate 68 from the Vocke Road intersection to the bridges at Clarysville removed most of the evidence of the railroad in that area, including the tunnels.

Cumberland Coal & Iron

The Cumberland Coal & Iron (CC&I) Company, chartered in 1850, purchased the Maryland Mining Company's mines and railroad property, including the village of Eckhart, in April 1852. The rail line was extended to the nearby Hoffman mines in 1859. Cumberland Coal & Iron was in turn acquired by the Consolidation Coal Company in 1870. CC&I Corporate records reside in the University of Michigan Library, and at the Hagley Museum in Delaware. In 1870, the Eckhart Branch Rail Road became part of the Cumberland & Pennsylvania (C&P) Railroad, also owned by Consolidation Coal. However, for a period of 20 years, from 1850-1870, the Eckhart Branch Rail Road operated independently of the C&P.

Consolidation Coal

The Consolidation Coal Company was established in 1864 and headquartered in the city of Cumberland, MD for the first 85 years (1864-1945). During this time, the company became the largest bituminous coal company in the eastern United States.

The company's origin began in the early 19th century when a 14-foot thick seam of bituminous coal referred to as The Big Vein was discovered in the Georges Creek Valley. This coal region became famous during the industrial revolution in the 19th century for its clean-burning low sulfur content that made it ideal for powering ocean steamers, riverboats, locomotives, steam mills, and machines shops. However, coal production did not really become important until the B&O Railroad reached Cumberland in 1842. In 1850, the opening of the Chesapeake & Ohio Canal from Georgetown, near Washington, DC, to Cumberland provided another route for coal shipments. Over 21 million short tons (2,000 pounds) of coal were transported on the

canal before it closed in 1923.

By 1850, almost 30 coal companies were mining the Georges Creek Valley, producing over 60 million tons of coal between 1854 and 1891. The Consolidated Coal Company was formed as a consolidation of the many coal mine and railroad companies of Western Maryland founded during the boom years. The Cumberland & Pennsylvania Railroad was owned by the Consolidation Coal Company.

Western Maryland's coal production rose about 1 million short tons in 1865, exceeded 4 million short tons by the turn of the century, and reached an all time high of about 6 million short tons in 1907. A small amount of the coal production in the early 1900s was premium blacksmithing coal that was specially processed and delivered in boxcars to customers throughout the United States and Canada.

Sharp declines in coal demand after 1920, reflecting downturns in the economy, recurrent labor problems and the extensive replacement of coal by petroleum products, led to further consolidations and mergers in the coal industry. As of 1999 the company has renamed itself to Consol Energy, reflecting the diversification of the business into other forms of energy. It is still in operation as of this writing.

Author's maternal Grandfather, Jake Ward, and his engine on the C&P Eckhart Branch.

The Eckhart Branch Railroad

The Eckhart Branch extended 12.4 miles from the B&O's Queen City Station in Cumberland to the Eckhart and Hoffman mines. Mileage is calculated from 0.0 at the Queen City Station. The section from Eckhart to Will's Creek was completed in 1846 by the Maryland Mining Company. This section included two tunnels. The C&P engines were restricted to a speed limit of 4 mph through the tunnels. This branch was also the location for a large "horseshoe" curve at Clarysville. The Hoffman Branch was constructed in 1859 by the Cumberland Coal & Iron Company. A tower marked Eckhart Junction on the main line, at the West end of the Narrows. The Eckhart Branch crossed Will's Creek on a brick arch bridge, which survived until removed in January of 1998.

The lower bridge is the one that has been removed. The bridge in the background was built for the Western Maryland Railway's Connellsville Extension, and is still in use today for the Western Maryland Scenic Railroad.

In this view, we are looking back towards Cumberland to the Narrows. The Eckhart Branch Bridge is to the right. The truss bridge from the other photo is behind us. The bridge in the background is the Pennsylvania Railroad in Maryland's connection. A steam locomotive is heading up the Eckhart Branch, past Eckhart Junction tower.

Westward beyond the Will's Creek bridge (mile post 2.3) was Lafferty's Siding, and sidings for a Sears warehouse, Feldsteins's Scrap yard, Cumberland Glass, and Boetcherville (Long, Md.) siding. At Cumberland Glass, the line crossed from the North to the South side of Rt. 40. The C&P swung south and climbed to cross Braddock Road at grade, then looped around and crossed Winchester Road on a reinforced concrete bridge. When this bridge was removed in the 1970's as part of the Winchester Road widening, the contractor vastly underestimated the extent of C&P's overdesign. The bridge took weeks to remove, being constructed of reinforced concrete, with steel "I" beams on 18" centers. Beyond the C&P bridge, rival Georges Creek and Cumberland Railroad crossed Winchester Road on a wooden trestle.

The Eckhart Branch continued behind the present Braddock Square Shopping Center, and followed roughly the path of the current Interstate 68. A water tank at Clarysville serviced the thirsty engines. This water tank survived into the 1950's. At Clarysville, the horseshoe curve arched up current Route 55 towards Midland. A wreck at this curve in 1917 affords us a unique opportunity for a look at the underside of a C&P engine.

At milepost 11.1, the tracks split to Hoffman Junction and the K&M Coal Company, and towards Eckhart. There was a two-stall engine house, shops, and a water tank. Mr. Michaels & son ran the engine house in the early part of the 20th century.

Eckhart was the location for Consolidation Mines 3, 4, and 10. The Hoffman line was torn out in 1949. Location of some of the earliest coal transportation on the line, Hoffman Mine No. 3 was once serviced by C&P's iron pot hopper cars. The last motive power on the line was Western Maryland decapods (wheel arrangement 2-10-0).

The B&O Railroad provided early motive power and rolling stock to the Allegany County coal shortlines. The B&O supplied at least eight Camel engines to the Maryland Mining Company, as evidenced by Winans' notes. These included B&O engines 161, 162, and 163, among others. In addition Ross Winans, among other builders, sold engines, tenders, and coal cars to the various mining companies. Passenger service was provided on the Eckhart Branch sometime before 1853, and the C&P continued to use a gravity passenger car on that line. The car was released in Eckhart, and allowed to roll down hill to Cumberland, under the control of a brakeman. The passenger car was later hauled back up the mountain at the end of a string of empty coal hoppers. Servicing, watering, and coaling facilities were located in Eckhart. The C&P maintained an engine house and servicing facilities here, and the foundations of these were still evident in 1999.

It is not known if this is a complete list of Eckhart Branch Motive Power. All of the listed engines except the first are of the *Camel* type. Hicks (ref. 23) recounts that the transfer records in the Maryland State archives (from MMC to CC&I) mention five engines. Two of these are Winans, but lighter in weight than the listed engines, and three are much lighter. Rankin mentions that the company motive power included three first class engines, two second class, and forty-one horses and mules. Rolling stock included sixty-eight iron hopper, gondola, scow, and passenger cars in 1853.

Eckhart Branch Motive Power Roster					
Builder	type	date	Name	company	disposition
1. unknown	2-2-2	-?-	*Enoch Pratt*	MMC	unknown
2. Winans No. 27	0-8-0	1849	*Eckhart*	MMC	rblt 1868, to C&P
3. Winans scrp. 1876	0-8-0	1849	*Mountaineer*	MMC	to C&P No. 28.
4. Winans	0-8-0	1851	*Fire King*	MMC	unknown
5. Winans	0-8-0	1852	*Black Monster*	CC&I **	to C&P No. 29
6. Winans renum. No. 30	0-8-0	1854	*Braddock*	CC&I	to C&P No. 31,
7. Winans	0-8-0	1853	*Cumberland*	CC&I	to C&P No. 30

Note for table:
** *Black Monster* has the same specifications as B&O No. 106 and 108. 19" x 22" cylinders, 43" drivers.

No pictures of any of these engines are known to exist. The Transfer records mention "2 engines of 23 ton's weight, 1 second-class coal/wood burner of 15 tons, 1 English make, American built of 15 tons, and 1 second class engine of 12 tons." The use of the *Enoch Pratt* is questionable, although it may be the 'American built of 15 tons' mentioned. A 2-2-2 wheel arrangement is unusual. The Robert Stephenson *Patentee* of 1833 was of this pattern. American manufacturers known to have copied Stephenson's work from Britain include Baldwin, Rogers, the Locks & Canal Company of Lowell, Ma., and the West Point Foundry. No extant records support the sales of an engine from any of these companies to Eckhart. The West Point Foundry had supplied the machinery to the Georges Creek Coal & Iron Company for the blast furnace at Lonaconing.

The *Eckhart* was a "second class" engine, with 17 inch cylinders. The *Braddock* was a first class engine, with 19 inch cylinders. Mr. Winans customarily gave a thirty day trial period to the purchasers. The engine *Mountaineer* was delivered on December 1, 1849, and accepted on Jan. 8, 1850. The engine *Cumberland* cost $11,000. and was delivered May 28, 1853. The engine *Fire King*, delivered 6/30/1851, came with a 4-wheel tender, holding 1 1/2 tons of coal, and 900 gallons of water. The engine *Frostburg* went into service on Nov. 20, 1852.

Service on the Eckhart Branch was hard, as evidenced by a series of correspondence with the Winans works in Baltimore in 1856. On June 16, 1856, CC&I ordered a replacement right-hand crosshead for the engine *Braddock*. The *Braddock* had gone into service on July 1, 1854. On September 24, they needed the same part for the engine *Eckhart*. The *Eckhart* had been placed into service on August 1, 1849. A frantic telegram on December 9, 1856, emphasizes the need for urgency for shipment of the replacement left-hand crosshead for the *Eckhart*. The engines *Black Monster* and *Cumberland* were at work at that time. The parts were delivered to the B&O Railroad at Cumberland. It is not known whether the repair work was done at Cumberland, or at Eckhart. The engine *Eckhart* was later rebuilt at the C&P shops in Mount Savage in 1868.

In addition, the B&O had at least eight Winans engines assigned to work on the Eckhart Branch railroad of the Maryland Mining Company near Cumberland.

At the opening ceremony of the rail line on Wednesday, May 13, 1846, a special train took the board of directors and guests from Cumberland to Eckhart, and returned. About two weeks later, an accident occurred on the line near the junction with the Mount Savage Rail Road, at the west end of the Narrows. A dozen passengers were injured when the brakes burned out on the train, and it overturned due to excessive speed. It was noted in a contemporary newspaper account that these were the same brakes commonly used on the Baltimore & Ohio line, but they were not adequate for the grades of the Eckhart Branch. Flooding in July of 1846 also caused extensive damage to the line's lower end.

A word on the proper name for the line is in order. The term *Eckhart Branch* seems to date from the later period of the 1870's. In a schedule published in the Frostburg Mining Journal, the line is referred to as the *Cumberland Branch*. It seems to depend on which end you started from. In the earliest accounts, the line is simply called the Maryland Mining Company Railway. During the Civil War, the rail line was probably used to transport supplies and patients to the Military Hospital facility at Clarysville.

From 1846 to 1870, the Winans camel engines of the Eckhart Railroad eased the heavy coal loads down the mountain, around the horseshoe curve, and through the tunnels to Cumberland.

These were the days of manual car brakes, and link-and-pin couplers. Brakemen ran across the tops of cars, in all sorts of weather, to manually set and release the handbrakes. Later, the camels would haul the empty coal hoppers and the lone passenger car back up the mountain in preparation for another day's work. The legacy of the Eckhart Branch railroad continued with the C&P, and with Western Maryland equipment into the 1950's.

The earliest coal cars were iron pot hoppers, such as this one belonging to the Consolidation Coal Company. They are bottom-dump. Examples survive in the Baltimore & Ohio Railroad Museum, in Baltimore, Maryland.

Later coal cars were of wooden construction on a steel frame. Much later, all-steel cars were introduced.

One of the limitations of the Eckhart Branch, besides the tunnel clearances, curves, and grade was the load capacity of the Will's Creek Bridge, at the West End of the Narrows.

The figure of merit on the Eckhart Branch was the number of empty hoppers that could be pulled uphill. This depends on the rolling resistance of the car, the grade resistance, and the curve resistance. The Winans engine could handle 40 hoppers, based on a tare weight of 3 tons for the Winans designed 6-wheel hoppers in use in 1854. The later engines would haul 55 ton capacity hoppers, of tare weight 20 tons. The capacity of a standard C&P class L engine would have been 21 cars.

The following page shows one of the Eckhart Branch tunnels.

C&P water tank at Lafferty's.

Railroad Accidents

The nature of the Eckhart Branch, with its steep grade and challenging curves, led to many accidents over the years.

Eckhart Branch Horseshoe Bend. Near Clarysvlle.. In this incident, the engine took the curve too fast, and fell over to the outside. Here, we have a unique view of the underside of a C&P engine, without having to venture into the pit in the Mount Savage shop.

Passenger Service

In 1872, according to the schedules published in the Frostburg Mining Journals, there were two round trips a day from Cumberland to Eckhart.

The Potomac Wharf Branch

The Potomac Wharf Branch was built by the Maryland Mining Company between 1846 and 1850, as an extension to the Eckhart Branch Railroad. The Potomac Wharf Branch crossed Will's Creek at Cumberland on a bridge (no longer present) just east of the present Route 40 road bridge. Some of the rail may still be seen near some billboards, and a gas station. The area near the creek end of present-day Wills Creek Avenue is known as City Junction, and had a water tank and a tower. The Potomac Wharf Branch was crossed by the Georges Creek & Cumberland Line. Rail was removed from the section west of the Valley Street crossing as late as 1990. In 1994, rail was removed from this area to maintain the Western Maryland Scenic Railroad, ex-GC&C line to Frostburg.

A classic wreck scene photo, circa 1860, shows the bridge collapsed into Will's Creek, with engine C. E. Detmold dangling into the creek. This was due to extensive flooding of Will's Creek which caused the bridge pillars to give way. This image indicates the branch and the facility were in use at least to this date. The original Potomac Wharf Branch bridge was a 203-foot deck plate girder structure, with two support pillars in the creek. Built in 1849, and rebuilt after the Detmold accident, it survived until the flood of 1936.

The Potomac Wharf branch carried coal to flat-bottom Potomac River boats, and later to canal boats, before the canal wharf facility was completed. There was a series of canal wharves at Cumberland.

Initially, canal boats could enter the Potomac River through the guard locks, and proceed upriver for some distance. The dam in the Potomac below the guard locks ensured that the Potomac was deeper at its junction with Will's Creek than it is today. The guard locks and the dam were removed as part of the Corps of Engineers Will's Creek flood control project for Cumberland in the 1950s.

The length of the Potomac Wharf branch was about 0.9 miles. The river terminus was the position where the present I-68 bridge passes over the B&O west end line. From City Junction, where the Wharf Branch crossed Will's Creek, the line proceeded eastward to meet the B&O tracks at the southern end of the B&O viaduct. The Potomac Wharf Branch was built on more of an upward slope than the GC&C, to meet the B&O tracks at viaduct level. It crossed Valley Street, and the south end of today's road bridge, at street level. The B&O line's roadbed is some 20 feet higher than the Western Maryland (Scenic) Line. East of Valley Street, some track and ties were still in place as late as 1994. Looking back from the B&O line, the junction of the Wharf Branch is easily seen.

B&O's Cumberland viaduct was built as a brick arch structure during the period 1849- 1851. The Wharf Branch line and the B&O main passed through the "deep cut". The deep cut provides the "West End" of the B&O with access to the Potomac River Valley, towards Keyser, and Grafton. The viaduct passes over city streets, Will's Creek, and the Western Maryland tracks (ex-GC&C, now used by the Western Maryland Scenic Railroad). The viaduct was double-tracked.The southern end of the cut is wide enough for triple track, and the bridges are designed for three tracks. They currently carry the CSX West End tracks. The C&P line merged into the B&O westernmost tracks, then crossed over to the easternmost track.

The wharf siding was about 1000 feet long, extending from the current Kelly Boulevard around to Will's Creek. The details of the facility and the method for loading coal from the rail cars to the canal boats are not known.The Potomac Wharf Branch was listed on the C&P valuation sheets in 1918, although it is doubtful it was in use for coal at that time.

Before crossing Wills Creek to City Junction, a spur of the Wharf Branch serviced the Wellington Glass Plant. The plant had been acquired from the National Glass Company.

The Potomac Wharf Branch was an early intermodal experiment to provide easy access for Western Maryland coal to the markets of the eastern seaboard. Although its useful life was short, it provided a needed short-term outlet for the export of the region's "black gold."

The Mines at Eckhart Mines

The mines in Eckhart included Console #4, Consol #10, Sullivan Brothers, and Ocean # 3 ½, among others

Console #4 worked the Big Vein at Eckhart. It is described by the mine inspectors as "one of the oldest mines in the Cumberland region, and is cut up in such a manner that ventilation and drainage is a serious proposition, making it very expensive and dangerous to operate." Horses were employed in the mine as late as 1915, and a large electric hoist motor hauled the coal to the surface, to be loaded into hoppers on the Eckhart Branch. In 1914, the mine employed 119 men, who produced over 80,000 tons of coal in 284 working days. James Weston was the Mine Foreman, and Hugo Rempel was the Assistant.

Consol #10 was an Eckhart mine that worked the Upper Sewickley (Tyson) seam. It employed small mules in the mine, and a large electric hoist motor. Once on the surface, the coal was put into mine cars, and went to the Consol #4 mine tipple by an endless rope arrangement. At the tipple, the coal was segregated from the Big Vein coal. Drainage and ventilation was reported to be good. For the year 1914, 112 men worked 281 days to produce almost 70,000 tons of coal. The Eckhart branch was restricted to 55 ton hoppers because of the curves and grades. This mine produced 1,272 hopper loads. Frank Myers was the Mine Foreman at this time, with John Kidwell as the Assistant.

The Sullivan Brothers Mine (John Sullivan, Superintendent, William J. Sullivan, Foreman) also worked the Upper Sewickley coal. In 1914 they employed 60 men and numerous mules to provide over 46,000 tons of coal, in 176 working days.

Ocean # 3 ½. mine employed 178 men and 7 mules, to output 440 tons per day.

The Mines at Hoffman

Originally called the Hoffman Hollow mine, this facility exploited the Pittsburgh Seam, or Big Vein. The exact date of its opening is not know, but it is thought to be around the time of the Civil War, but could have been as early as 1852. It was renamed Ocean #3 in 1897, and Consol #3 in 1913. It went by the name of Hoffman #3 after 1938. The mine operated until 1947, and was abandoned in 1948.

Cumberland Coal & Iron opened the mine on land it purchased in the early 1850's. The first comprehensive report on coal mines in Maryland in 1877 mentions the Hoffman Mine in conjunction with the nearby Astor Mine, which had an underground fire in 1862. such fires were common, as fires were used to provide ventilation before mechanical systems were employed for this. In 1877, the Hoffman mine extended 1,300 feet. In 1881, the slope extended 3,100 feet, and the mine was connected to Consol Mine #1 in Ocean. The mine reached its maximum length of over 7,000 feet in 1898, when it was producing 1,200 tons of coal per day.

The Hoffman Mine was always plagued by water seepage, and expensive pumping operations were required to continue the operations. As other mines were connected to Hoffman (Console # 7 and #11, as well as #1) they tended to drain through Hoffman. By 1900, the problem reached a crisis point. From 1904 to 1909, Consol Coal had a three mile drainage tunnel dug from the bottom of the Hoffman Mine to Braddock's Run near Clarysville. The tunnel worked so well it allowed the re-opening of the Borden Shaft mine, Consol #12, in 1913.

The peak production year at the Hoffman mine was 1913, when it produced 447,252 tons of coal, all going down the Eckhart Branch to Cumberland. There were three mine openings, and the mine sprawled across over 800 acres. This mine relied on a compressed air facility on the surface to supply power to pumps, drills, and locomotives. In 1914, the mine employed almost 600 men, and produced almost 440,000 tons of coal in 291 days. The Mine Foreman was Jenkins Daniels, with Patrick Kenney and Chas. Shields as Assistants. During its lifetime, the Hoffman mine extracted around 5,280,000 tons of coal

The Hoffman Drainage Tunnel

The Hoffman Drainage tunnel was an engineering triumph of its age. Built in the period 1903 through 1906, it was hand-driven through solid rock for 2 miles to provide an outlet for water that was flooding the coal mines. The water had proven to be too much for the steam pumps, and coal production was stagnating. After an engineering survey of the tunnel project by the Consolidation Coal Company, a contract was let to Mr. Phillip Jenkins, Sr. of Wales. Work was begun from both ends in November of 1903 by Jenkins' four sons, William, Edward, James, and Phillip, Jr.

This work was different from coal mining. The Jenkins crew were familiar with hard rock mining from their native Wales. To speed progress, a shaft was sunk 181 feet deep inside Hoffman Mine number 3. From the bottom of this, the men dug in both directions, giving 4 working faces.

The tunnel proceeds in a straight line, except for an 18 degree turn located some 400 feet from the east (exit) portal. The tunnel is a uniform 8 feet in height and width, and follows a downgrade of some 1/3 percent. This put the exit 40 feet lower than the drainage area in the mine, more than adequate for adequate flow. The excavation work proceeded in three shifts per day, involving blasting through hard rock. Working conditions were described as "wretched" due to the cold water seepage. The men worked in rubber waders. A pump was added near the exit, at the horseshoe curve of the Eckhart Branch of the C&P railroad, to help control the flow. The miners used lard oil lamps for illumination. Drilling for the blasts was done by hand, with a three man crew. The excavated rock was removed through Hoffman number 3 mine, and dumped on the slate banks.

Later, a mule was lowered into the central shaft, and served there for 6 months. William Jenkins was in charge of the dynamite, and his brother James was supervisor of the digging. They stayed in the nearby Clarysville Inn while the work was proceeding. During the dig, there were only 2 accidents, and only 1 man died. The project cost $300,000.

The tunnel was punched through on Saturday, July 21, 1906 at 9 pm. It was found to be off by less than three inches. The Frostburg Mining Journal of September. 15, 1906, proclaimed, "The Great Work Complete." Inside the mines, the pumps were silenced, and gravity took over to lower the water level. It is estimated that 9,000,000 gallons of water were drained in 24 hours.

The impact on the coal workings was immediate. A tremendous amount of coal, previously inaccessible, was now available. Over 50 additional men were working the coal. In addition, conditions in the mines improved. Thirteen miles of mine drainage ditches fed the tunnel. Observers noted in the *Cumberland News* of 1906 that the volume of water carried by Braddock Run was ten times greater after 2 months of the tunnel opening. The red coloration and the odor of sulfur was noted as far downstream as Wills Creek in the Narrows.

Tunnel maintenance was maintained until about 1953. The mines stopped working around 1960. As of February 2000, the concrete portal arch at the east or drainage end is still standing. The overburden upstream for some 30 meters is gone, and some timbering can be seen in the stream bed. The water seems to emerge upward from the end of a blind canyon, and flow through the arch. The inscription on the arch can still be clearly read: "1903-1906, Hoffman Drainage Tunnel, Length 2 miles."

The east end of the tunnel, with its associated concrete arch is located next of one of the bridge abutments that carried the C&P horseshoe curve over the creek at that point. The water flow in Feb. 2000 was quite brisk, with no obvious smell of sulfur, but with a decided red tinge to the water.

The Lonaconing Residency

Introduction

In the early 19th century, a 14-foot thick seam of bituminous coal referred to historically as *The Big Vein* was discovered in the Georges Creek Valley. This coal region would become famous for its clean-burning low sulfur content that made it ideal for powering ocean steamers, river boats, locomotives, and steam mills, and machines shops. By 1850, almost 30 coal companies were mining the Georges Creek Coal, producing over 60 million tons of coal between 1854 to 1891, with 5,000 men working underground. In the census of 1860, over 90% of the miners could read and write.

The Town of Lonaconing was located centrally in the Georges Creek Valley, between Frostburg at the north, and Westernport at the south. Both towns at the extremes had rail junctions. There were plans to extend the canal through Westernport. Lonaconing became the largest among the dozen or so towns along the Georges Creek, serving as a manufacturing center, a home for companies and miners, and a major retail center. Today Lonaconing is a town of some 1,200, still the largest among the Georges Creek communities.

The Companies

This section will discuss the company's that were instrumental in iron manufacturing in Lonaconing.

Georges Creek Coal & Iron Company

The Georges Creek Coal & Iron (GCC&I) Company was formed in 1835, and chartered in the State of Maryland on March 29, 1836. It was backed by British Capital, and managed by investors from New York. The company bought 11,000 acres along Georges Creek from the locals, mostly land grants for Revolutionary War service. The president was John Henry Alexander, who had served as the Maryland State Engineer. He was aware of the vast coal and iron deposits in Western Maryland. His partner was Philip C. Tyson.

John H. Alexander (1812-1867)

Alexander was born in Annapolis, Maryland. He graduated from St. John's College, and spent the next 4 years studying law. He also attended medical courses in Baltimore, but chose to go to work for the Baltimore & Susquehanna Railroad doing surveys and maps. He was appointed Chief Engineer of Maryland in 1833. He worked on the first complete map of Maryland, and got interested in potential canal routes and coal deposits, for "internal improvement." He resigned from the State, and co-founded the Georges Creek Coal and Iron Company with Mr. Tyson. He laid out the main street of Lonaconing in1837.

He was also Professor of Physics at the University of Maryland, Professor of Civil Engineering at the University of Pennsylvania, and a member of an International Commission on weights and measures. He was a fellow of the American Philosophical Society. He's mentioned in Who's Who in America, Historical Volume. He was the Chair of the Physics Department at St. James College, Maryland, and received a Doctorate there.

His papers (1824-1857) are preserved at the University of Maryland Libraries archives, and at the Maryland Historical Society in Baltimore. He was published in many different fields.

Philip T. Tyson

A Geologist and Chemist, he was a partner in the Georges Creek Coal and Iron Company. He was the State Agricultural Chemist in Maryland, and discovered significant dinosaur fossils in the Arundel Formation in Bladensburg, Maryland, in an iron pit. The Arundel clay is know for its iron ore, and Lower Cretaceous fossils. Mr. Tyson's find was a sauropod, now the Maryland State Dinosaur.

The 1836 prospectus of the Company outlined a plan to build four coke-fired blast furnaces powered by steam engines. There was also to be a rolling mill, puddling furnaces, steam hammers, and a foundry. The business plan was to produce and sell bar iron, railroad rail, and large castings. The projected workforce was 1,000 men. The plan targeted rail for the B&O Railroad, pushing west from Baltimore. The Lonaconing facility would have transportation access down the Georges Creek to Westernport, Maryland and Piedmont, Virginia, to the railroad and the C&O Canal. The estimated investment cost was $167,930. The technology came from Wales, and Alexander said, "the time will come when ...the Western County of Maryland shall be looked upon as the Wales of North America." Good plan, if they could pull it off. Within months, the investors flocked in, eventually numbering 22. Three thousand shares were offered, at $100. each. The Company was politically well connected in Baltimore and Annapolis. Things were going well.

As the ex-Maryland Geologist, Alexander know a lot about mines, and about iron making. He saw Wales as a model. His vision was to recreate the Merthyr Tydfil facility in the Georges Creek Valley.

Between 1837 and 1839, the new company built an iron furnace in the Welsh pattern at Lonaconing. The furnace, fueled by coke, went into blast in 1839. This was a first for the United States. The abundance of good coal and decent iron ore, like in Wales, made all the difference. Wages were twice the going rate in Wales. Thus, British iron, produced in Wales, was available in America for half the cost of the domestic product.

Not all the pieces fell into place. The railroad down the valley came too late to haul the furnace's product. A canal down the Georges Creek was discussed. An economic depression in the country in 1839-1840 didn't help. The efficiency of scale that would have been achieved by the planned multiple furnaces never happened. The furnace produced 1,860 tons of pig iron in its last active year, 1855. It was then shut down, and abandoned. The C&O Canal never got past Cumberland. The railroad portion of the operation was sold to the C&P in 1863.

Other key figures in the Georges Creek Iron & Coal company include:

Patrick MaCauly – Baltimore businessman, President of American Life Insurance and Trust, investor in GCC&I.

Richard Wilson - Baltimore businessman, Secretary of American Life Insurance and Trust, investor in GCC&I.

Louis McLean - President of the Baltimore and Ohio Railroad (1836), Secretary of the Treasury under Jackson, investor in GCC&I. He lead the construction of the B&O Railroad westward from Baltimore.

John Steele – Welshman, supervisor for the coal miners, and for coke production.

David Hopkins - Welsh Founder, in charge of building the blast furnace.

John Phillips – One of the "Keepers of the Furnace," supervising filling and tapping.

John Thomas - One of the "Keepers of the Furnace," supervising filling and tapping.

Charles B. Shaw – American engineer and Works superintendent.

David Hopkins – Welsh workforce leader. He got the blast furnace built and operating in 18 months.

In 1910, Georges Creek Coal and Iron became the Georges Creek Coal Company, and operates to this day.

The Georges Creek Railroad

The B&O reached Piedmont, across the Potomac River from Westernport, in July of 1851. In September of that year, the railroad construction began up the Georges Creek. The railroad was opened on May 9, 1853. In June, a total of 1,061 tons of coal were shipped. In all of 1855, 225,000 tons of coal were shipped, sometimes in 102 car trains. Iron ore or cast iron did not figure into the shipments. In 1856, the line was extended from Lonaconing northward to connect with the C&P from Frostburg. The Georges Creek Coal & Iron

Company's 9.2 mile railroad was acquired by the C&P on October 23, 1863. The shops and engine house at Lonaconing were used until 1867. These were located just north of where the road to Dan's Mountain State Park merges with State Route 36, at Water Station Road, north of Lonaconing. Interestingly, this section of line still saw use in 1998 for on-demand coal service. In 1991, the Georges Creek subdivision of CSX hauled 195,197 tons of coal over this line, as compared with the 225,000 tons by the Georges Creek Rail Road in 1855. The line is still in place, but currently out of service.

Locomotive builders Baldwin and Smith & Perkins sold engines and rolling stock to the Georges Creek Company. Ross Winans of Baltimore sold wheels and axles to the GCC&I for mine cars. Passenger service was provided on the Georges Creek Railroad with their 2-6-0 engine. A list of motive power for the Georges Creek Rail Road has been compiled, but it is not known if this is a complete list. All of the listed engines were transferred to Cumberland & Pennsylvania Railroad ownership, as part of the buyout. No pictures of the 2-6-0 or 0-6-0 engines are known to exist. Locomotives were generally named after geographical references, or persons of significance. Mr. A. H. Stump was the President of the Georges Creek Coal & Iron Company in 1884. A.H. Stump & Sons were founders and machinists in Baltimore in 1878. None of these locomotives are know to have survived.

Roster of Motive Power of the Georges Creek Railroad					
Name	Type	Builder	Date	Notes	
Disposition					
A.H. Stump	2-6-0	S & P	1852		C&P No. 5, scrp 1875
Georges Creek	0-8-0	Baldwin	1853	Builder number 521	C&P No. 6, scrp 1876
Lonaconing	0-6-0	Baldwin	1853	Builder number 558	C&P No. 7, scrp 1874

S&P stands for Smith & Perkins, locomotive manufacturers of Alexandria, VA.

Surveys were made by Detmold in 1846 to construct a railroad to Clarysville (Claery's Tavern) to connect with the line of the Maryland Mining Company Railroad from Eckhart to Cumberland. This was never accomplished.

Lonaconing Ocean Coal Mining and Transportation Company

The company was authorized in 1853 by the Maryland State Legislature. It was formed by William H. Aspinwall, Edward Cunard, Auguste Belmont, Joseph B. Varnum, Jonathan Meredith, Edward J. Woolsey, and James L. Graham. They were authorized to mine coal, and to build railroads as needed in Allegany County, or purchase or lease them. They could own and operate steam or sailing vessels. They could condemn land they needed for the railroad projects. They were authorized to collect transportation tolls of three cents per ton-mile on merchandise, and two cents per mile for passengers.

If you wanted to set up a mining and transportation company in 1853, it would be hard to pull together a better set of directors:

William Henry Aspinwall was an American businessman. In 1832, he became president of the "Howland & Aspinwall" merchant firm, which had been founded by his cousin and expanded trade to South American, China, Europe, the Mediterranean, and the East and West Indies. In 1848 he founded the Pacific Mail Steamship Company. He then promoted the Panama Railroad across the Isthmus. He retired in 1856 but remained active as a philanthropist He was a founder of the Society for the Prevention of Cruelty to Animals and of the Metropolitan Museum of Art.

Edward Cunard was the son of Sir Samuel Cunard of Halifax, Nova Scotia. Sir Samuel founded the Cunard Line, a British shipping Company, which still operates with a Headquarters in London.

August Belmont, Sr. was born in the German Province of Hesse. He immigrated to New York in 1837 after becoming the American representative of the Rothschild banking house in Frankfurt.

He founded August, Belmont & Co. believing that he could replace the defunct American Agency with his company. It was an instant success, and Belmont was able to straighten out the Rothschild interests in the United States between 1837 and 1842.

On receiving his American citizenship, he married Caroline Slidell Perry, daughter of Commodore Matthew Perry.

Joseph B. Varnum was associated with the Mt. Savage Iron Company, and the railroads.

Jonathan Meredith (b.1784), was a commercial lawyer in Baltimore; council for the Bank of the United States and the Bank of Baltimore. Had the acquaintance of every President from Washington to Grant.

Edward J. Woolsey, of Woolsey Mansion, Astoria, Long Island, was a Director of the Delaware & Hudson Canal and Railroad Co., 1860.

James Lorimer Graham (1804-1882) was an American lawyer specializing in real estate. He was president of the Metropolitan Insurance Company in New York City.

The Lonaconing Ocean Coal Mining and Transportation Company changed its name, with the concurrence of the Maryland State Legislature, to the Ocean Steam Coal Company in 1872. Ocean became the name of a small community near the mines.

Key People

Christian Edward Detmold, (2/2/1810-7/2/1887)

Detmold was a major figure in the Lonaconing Iron Furnace. A civil engineer by training, born in Hanover, Germany, Detmold had entered the U.S. at age 16, en route to Brazil to join the Army, but decided to stay instead. He did surveys for a railroad in Charleston, S.C., won a $500. prize for a horse treadmill car from the Charleston & Hamburg Railroad & Canal Co., and worked for the U.S. War Department on the construction of Fort Sumter.

From 1845 to 1852, Detmold was involved in iron production at Lonaconing. He was responsible for the construction of the tram road in 1847 from Lonaconing to Clarysville. (Sometimes referred to as the Detmold Tramway, or Detmold Railroad). This line connected with the Eckhart Branch Railroad, constructed by the Maryland Mining Company. Detmold leased the furnace, overhauled the boilers, and rebuilt the engine house. The furnace went back into blast in May 1846, and Detmold had a flourishing business by 1847. He was producing 2,500 tons of pig iron annually. The Georges Creek company, perhaps jealous of his success, declined to renew his lease. He moved on to direct construction of the Exhibit of Industry, at the Crystal Palace in New York which opened in July 1853. He held several patents including one dated 1858, when he was living in New Jersey for a "mode of securing the ends of railway bars." His 1843 patent, modified and reissued in 1845 (when he was living in New York) was for a reheating process to take cast iron the next step. C. E. Detmold is remembered by having both a town, and a C&P engine named after him.

James Millholland

James A. Millholland was as a railroad executive, serving as General Manager and later President of the George's Creek and Cumberland Railroad in Cumberland, Maryland. His father, James Millholland Senior (1812-1875) was born in Baltimore. He was a railway master mechanic and particularly well known for his invention of many railway mechanisms. His association with the Philadelphia and Reading Railroad Company as master machinist spanned fifty years in the early development of the American railroad. The senior Millholland's inventions and contributions include the cast-iron crank axle, wooden spring, plate girder bridge, poppet throttle, anthracite firebox, water grate, drop frame, and steel tires. He was also an early user and advocate of the superheater, the feed-water heater, and the injector. Several of his innovations were adopted as standard practice by the railroad industry.

Lonacona

Lonacona, or George Washington Cresap, was the son of Nemacolin, a famous Delaware Chief. The town of Lonaconing was named for Lonacona. Georges Creek was also named for him. Lonacona died around 1790 in the home of his friend Dan, and he is buried in the Cresap Cemetery in Rawlings, MD. Lonacona's daughter Teresa married William Workman of Mt. Savage, MD. Later, William moved his family to Kerens, WV. (From the article "Chief Nemacolin--A Delaware Indian Headman" by Alma Irene King-Finney.)

The Facility

By 1850, almost 30 coal companies were mining the Big Vein, producing over 60 million tons of coal between 1854 to 1891, with 5,000 men working underground. In the census of 1860, over 90% of the miners could read and write, because the Company built schools and churches for the workforce and their families. After that, large numbers of skilled iron workers were lured from Wales to the wilderness of Western Maryland. By 1838, a sailing ship left Wales, with 73 passengers for Lonaconing. It took 10 weeks to Baltimore. Advertisements in the Baltimore Newspaper sought all kinds of labor. The

Town and facility were operated, according to the "Rules of the Lonaconing Residency." This was at least particularly due to the friction among the various ethnic groups, who brought quarrels from the old world. And perhaps also due to American moonshine. The Rules banned fighting, drinking alcohol, and firing guns. Another problem was that the common language was bad English, a second language for most of the workmen.

The Town of Lonaconing is located centrally in the Georges Creek Valley, between Frostburg at the north, and Westernport at the south. Both towns had rail junctions. There were plans to extend the C&O canal through Westernport. Lonaconing became the largest among the dozen or so towns along the Georges Creek, serving as a manufacturing center, a home for companies and miners, and a major retail center. Today Lonaconing is a town of some 1,200, still the largest among the Georges Creek communities. The furnace still stands in a town park, and the office building of the Georges Creek Coal & Iron Company is still adjacent, now used as a residence.

Construction

The furnace, modeled on the Welsh pattern, was built with locally quarried sandstone. It was to be fifty feet high, fifty feet on a side at the base, and 25 feet wide at the top – a truncated pyramid. It was built against the side of a hill, and charged from the top. The liquid metal would be tapped at the bottom. It could be in continuous blast, as long as the raw materials were available. The interior chamber is 5.5 feet square at the top, and 14.5 feet wide at the widest point, near the bottom. Each face of the furnace had a 16-foot wide brick arch. Cast iron beams were incorporated into the archways. The furnace expanded and compressed during the blast process, as it heated and cooled, and metal stiffening was needed. This took the form of wrought iron bar or rod. At the end, these were looped, and iron wedges pushing against large iron washers locked the bars in place. Some of the bars were threaded for large iron nuts. These can be seen on the structure today. All of the iron pieces for the furnace were shipped in.

A tram road was cut for the stone to reach the building site from the quarries above the furnace. At first, a large sled was used, but was replaced with wheeled ones later. These were of timber construction, built on site.

A large inclined plane was built to supply coal to the furnace. A pulley system with chains and a large drum at the top allowed loaded cars to pull up empty ones. The iron chain came from England. Ross Winans of Baltimore supplied the iron hardware for the cars, such as wheels and axles. Local farmers rented out their teams and wagons to the company. The masonry contractor was from Pennsylvania, and used local labor to augment his masons. Wooden templates were used to ensure proper placement of the stones for the interior of the furnace. Iron reinforced wooden cranes, and a windlass were used to set the stones. Mortar was produced on site from burned limestone. Lime kilns were built to a French pattern to produce the mortar. Eventually 28 kilns were built.

Bricks, produced on site, were used for the arches, the chimneys, two hot air furnaces, and the furnace for the steam boilers. A Baltimore brick maker lead the team, with several journeymen and lots of manual laborers. The carpenters built the brick molds, and large tables to hold them. There were four kilns. In 1838, the Company consumed a million bricks.

Firebricks were going to be used to line the furnace, but the local fire clay was difficult to work with, and the furnace was eventually lined with sandstone to keep on schedule.

One key ingredient of a blast furnace is the blast. The company bought the necessary machinery from the West Point Foundry in New York City. The machinery went by ship from New York to Georgetown, then by the C&O canal to Williamsport, which was, at that time, the end of the line. Here, the parts were loaded on wagons for the final leg of the journey. The canal charged $3.50 per ton to transport the twenty tons of machinery parts. Only the boilers made it to Lonaconing before the canal froze in the winter of 1837.

Ten additional wagon loads from Williamsport arrived at the site in November.

The blast machinery featured a 60-horsepower steam engine fed by five boilers. The steam cylinders were 18 inches in diameter, and 8 feet long. The system operated at a pressure of 50 pounds per square inch (psi). The steam cylinder drove a blast cylinders 5 feet in diameter, and 8 feet long. This forced about 3500 cubic feet per minute of air at 2.5 psi through the system. A very large iron regulator smoothed the air flow from the reciprocating cylinder. The air flowed through a series of pipes in the boiler furnaces and was heated to 600 degrees F. The heated air then entered the blast furnace through two big water cooled nozzles called *tuyeres*. When the water supply failed, the furnace had to be operated with a less efficient cold blast. The first run of good iron came from the furnace on May 17, 1839. By May 23, the furnace was producing six tons per day. Seven tons of coal were required to produce one ton of the cast metal.

The piping for heating the blast came from three Baltimore foundries, including Ross Winans'. Water pipes were made from wood, hollowed logs, and supplied water for the boilers, and to cool the tuyeres. A dam was constructed, with a sand-filled filter. The blast pipes were sealed at the joints with lead, which limited the temperature of the blast to below 620 degrees.

The need for plank lumber for the buildings and houses lead the Company to construct a sawmill capable of producing up to 20,000 board feet per day. It could also produce shingles and lath. The company bought some 20,000 square feet of zinc plate for roofing, from Baltimore.

The company was betting on getting good access to cheap transportation, and bought land in Cumberland near where the canal would be for a wharf facility. Surveys were done for three possible paths for a railroad from Lonaconing to the canal basin at Cumberland. But, in 1839 the Canal was stalled, and still had 50 miles to go.

The Company needed a good access road at least to the National Road. Several routes were surveyed, one through Pompey Smash to Clarysville. The

Town of Frostburg wanted the road and its business, so it offered financial incentives to the Company. This is the current Maryland Route 936.

If you drive south on Route 36 today to Lonaconing, the iron furnace is to the right, in a city park. To it's right is the Georges Creek Coal and Iron office building, now apartments. This is all that remains of a large industrial facility. Besides the furnace, there was a foundry with drop hammer, a refinery forge with its own 4 ton hammer, several puddling furnaces, power shears, and puddler rollers. One the basic facility was built, the furnaces and mills could make additional parts for the facility so they did not have to be imported from elsewhere. There was a water-powered sawmill, and a molding house, where the molds for the castings were made. Two big steam engines drove the blast cylinder. Coal and iron ore and limestone were brought from the mines along tramways lined with cast rail made at the facility. Cola was processed into coke in ovens; limestone was ground into powder for fluxing and to make cement, and iron ore was ground into smaller pieces. The facility was in operation 24x7.

Operations

Above the furnace were numerous beds of coal and iron ore, as well as the water supply. Veins of iron ore to about a foot in thickness were beside coal in the 14 ¼ foot wide "big vein." Their were five underground iron mines, and one coal mine. Some open pit mining was also done. Even common labor was becoming hard to find, as the C&O Canal and the B&O Railroad were both under construction. At a yard at the top of the furnace, the ore was roasted to remove impurities, and the coal was coked. The limestone flux was broken into small pieces. All of the charges were weighed, and there were precise portions of the raw materials, as directed by the iron master.

There were 200 men at work at the facility, including 140 miners, 38 furnace hands, and carpenters, blacksmiths, and laborers. Company housing was provided, with work done by the eventual tenants, and by company carpenters. The two-story company store was on Main Street. The store was run by Alexander's brother William. Materials arrived by wagon from Baltimore in 9 days. The company requested a post office be set up in

Lonaconing in 1837. Mail to Baltimore took two days. The company built a school and an Episcopal Church. The church was up on the hill, behind the furnace. Services were conducted in Welsh.

Beginning in August of 1837, the Company began keeping a daily business Journal. We are fortunate that these volumes survive.

The furnace was finished, and charged on May 9, 1839. May 17 saw the first iron made in a coke-fired furnace in America appear. The Company reportedly spend $78. on beer. After 10 days of operation, the tuyeres burned out, and piping was laid to supply water to cool them.

In the late 1830's and early 1840s' the facility was producing 13 tons of quality pig iron per day. There was very little local need for more iron. Shipping by wagon was slow and costly, $120 per ton. The company scaled back and finally ceased production, and began using its stockpile of iron to produce rails. It went into maintenance mode. The furnace was leased to Christian Detmold in 1846, and continued in operation. He gave it a go until 1852. In 1854, the Company brought the furnace back into operation. Sixty tons per week were being produced. In 1856, the furnace was shut down for good. Costs were high, due to labor and transportation. It wasn't working out.

The furnace complex at Lonaconing was visited by the Superintendent of Construction for the B&O, Mr. Casper Wever, Esq., in June of 1839. Shortly afterwards, the shareholders of the C&O Canal visited. With the furnace up and operating, the facility expansion plans included a forge and rolling mill. However, these were never built. The company began to concentrate on the railroad to meet with the canal and the railroad at Westernport. By 1850, surveys were complete.

The furnace sat idle for many years. It was named to the National Register of Historic Places, and was rehabilitated and stabilized by the firm of Meyers and D'Aleo, Inc. of Baltimore. It still sits in the City Park in Westernport.

The Georges Creek & Cumberland Railroad

Besides the C&P and the trolley, the residents of the Georges Creek could opt for the Georges Creek and Cumberland Railroad passenger service. The depot was on Scotch Hill.

GC&C passenger stations were located at Cumberland, Vale Summit, Midland, and Lonaconing. The station at Lonaconing was located up the hill behind the iron furnace, and was reportedly inconvenient to reach. The right of way of the line is still evident in this area, but no rails remain. The GC&C used the Hay Street Station in Cumberland, and made a passenger stop at Mechanic Street.

The GC&C rostered a 4-6-0 passenger engine. The GC&C had several passenger cars, including an observation car with open sides. This car was popular for political outings and picnic excursions, but not in the winter.

The January 18, 1887 published schedule shows two trains per day from Cumberland to Lonaconing (except Sundays). If you took the 10:45 AM from Lonaconing, you could lunch in Cumberland before catching the 1:15 PM to New York over the Pennsylvania Railroad. This express service would arrive in New York at 7:10 AM the next day. There was checked baggage service on this line.

The GC&C motive power all came from the Pittsburgh Locomotive and Car Works. Ten engines were rostered. There were nine engines of the 2-8-0 wheel arrangement, and a 4-6-0 passenger engine. All of the engines went to the Western Maryland, and all were reported scrapped between 1914 and 1917. For rolling stock, the GC&C rostered predominately coal hoppers; two hundred being listed for the year 1884. In addition, the 1884 Poor's lists two box cars, and 10 platform cars. The various ICC valuations list 24 GC&C cabooses for 1911 and 1912, and 20 for the year 1913. The GC&C also had several passenger cars, including an open-sided observation car.

The GC&C was big on trestles. During construction of the line, a single contract for 1.5 million feet of pine trestling lumber was let. Bridge *42* was the Winchester Road Viaduct, which crossed just south of the C&P Bridge. Uphill of the line's two tunnels was Bridge 50, the Percy Hollow Trestle. Past Clarysville was Needham's Viaduct, also called Bridge 81. Clises Run Viaduct, Bridge 115, at Cabin Run was a major structure. This was of wooden construction first, then later replaced with a steel structure. The stone abutments still exist.

Bridge 137, the Midland viaduct, bisected the town. The stone abutment for the northern end can still be seen between Routes 936 and 55, at the northern end of the town.

Beyond Midland, there was a bridge over Douglas Run, the stone ends of which can also still be seen. A turntable was located at Midland Junction. Bridges were necessary at Mile post 16 and 17 to cross and recross Georges Creek, the road, and the line of the Cumberland and Westernport Electric railway. Bridge 06 crossed the Pine Hill Plane. Bridge 20, the Jackson Wye viaduct, was located on the Jackson Branch, near milepost 19. A trestle was necessary over Castle Run at milepost 20, on the branch to the Koontz mine.

Mount Savage, Iron Empire

Mount Savage is a community in Allegany County with a current population is 2200. Drive through the Town of Mount Savage today, and you would probably only remember it for the dog-leg turn and the narrow main street.

It was in 1844 that Mount Savage was put on the nation's map with the rolling of the first iron rail in the United States. After this claim to fame, Mount Savage became the fifth largest city in Maryland. Today, no more iron is made at Mount Savage, nor do locomotives roll out of the shops. Little coal is mined, but the fire brick and refractory materials industry continue.

Alternate (unofficial) names for Mount Savage have been Arnold Settlement, Corriganville, Jennings, Jennings Run, Jennons (sic) Run, Jennings Post Office, and Lulworth.

Many buildings in Mount Savage are on the Register of Historic Places. The Mount Savage Historic District comprises 189 buildings, structures, and sites within the 19th and 20th century industrial community northwest of Cumberland. The resources within the district reflect the community's development as a center of the iron, coal, brick, and railroad industries from the 1830s to the early 20th century. A broad variety of domestic, commercial, religious, and industrial buildings and structures represent all phases of the town's development during this period. The town's commercial center is located on Main Street, and consists primarily of two and three-story commercial buildings dating from the turn of the 20th century. Most are of frame construction, but some are built with glazed brick, an architectural novelty produced in local brick works. A rich collection of domestic architecture is concentrated to the north, east, and southwest of the commercial area. Most of the houses are 1 1/2 or 2-story frame buildings, simplified interpretations of popular turn-of-the-20th-century styles, such as the Bungalow-influenced houses which line New Row and Foundry Row. Late-19th century fashions are represented by notable frame Gothic houses, an Eastlake-influenced brick example, and a group of large frame Queen Anne houses. Several vertical-board duplexes overlook the former site of the Maryland and New York Iron and Coal Company operations, established in

1839. This site is currently occupied by the Mount Savage Refractories brick works, the present descendant of the fire-brick industry which has operated continuously in town since the mid 19th century.

The Mount Savage Historic District is significant for its association with the industrial development of the Western Maryland region, and for its rich architectural resources representing a wide variety of types and styles of domestic, commercial, religious, and industrial buildings and structures reflecting all phases of the community's development from the mid 19th to the early 20th centuries. The vertical-board duplexes on Old Row are especially noteworthy as possibly the earliest examples of workers' housing remaining in the region.

The Companies

This section discusses the various 19th Century companies operating in Mount Savage.

Maryland & New York Iron & Coal Company (1838-1847)

On March 12, 1838, The Maryland and New York Iron & Coal Company was incorporated by Louis Howell, Benjamin B. Howell, and Henry Howell. The Howell Brothers of New York were bankers and brokers who could arrange for money for projects with a large anticipated rate of return. Benjamin Howell visited the Mount Savage area sometime before 1839, and liked what he saw. He ventured to England to gather Capital for an Iron Works; he succeeded to the extent of $600,000. The company was authorized to build a railroad from its mines at Mount Savage to the C&O Canal and the B&O Railroad at Cumberland by the terms of the charter: Both the B&O Railroad and the C&O Canal were on their way to Cumberland at this time.

Howell probably read Alexander's reports on the Lonaconing Project, picked out the ideas that worked, and discarded those that didn't. He build the Mount Savage facility in an area with the right raw materials (iron, limestone, and fireclay), but also with an existing community of potential workers, and infrastructure. Also, a rail connection to Cumberland was considered from Day 1. Howell purchased 3,700 prime acres from Andrew Bruce for $33,000. 1839 saw the construction of the first furnace. Until the railroad was completed to Cumberland, the right-of-way was used as a road, for horse-drawn wagons.

Louis Howell had vast land holdings and mines in Allegany County. The State charter allowed the Company to build or acquire railroads, as long as they did not interfere with the B&O, or the C&O Canal. They were also required to erect an Iron Works, and produce 1000 tons of pig, cast, or bar iron in one year. It is important to remember that when the legislature granted the rights to build a railroad, they included the right to condemn and acquire private land if it were needed to build the line.

61

Other investors included Joseph Weld, Thomas Weld Blundell, John Folliott Powell, Robert Samuel Palmer of the U.K., and several other American investors.

Louis Howell was lost at sea on the side wheel steamship *President* in 1841. The ship was at the time the largest steamship ever built. She was on her third crossing of the Atlantic. One could speculate that Mr. Howell was heading to England to raise Capital for his venture.

The State charter says:

"And be it enacted, That for the purpose of enabling said company to transport the produce of the mines and of the counties through which their rail road shall pass, on the cheapest and most expeditious manner, the said company and the president and directors thereof shall be, and hereby are respectively invested with all and singular the rights, profits, powers, privileges, authorities, immunities and advantages fur the surveying, locating, establishing and constructing a rail road and its necessary appurtenances, beginning the same at the mines of the said company and running to a convenient point or points on the basin or canal of the Chesapeake and Ohio Canal Company, at or near the town of Cumberland, in this State, and for the using, preserving and controlling the said rail road, its necessary vehicles and appurtenances and every part thereof, or borrowing money on the credit of the company for its lawful purposes; provided, that no such borrowing of money shall imply a right to borrow or purchase the stocks of the State, or any other description of property whatever, which by the act, and more particularly the fifteenth section thereof, incorporating the Baltimore and Ohio Rail Road Company, and its several supplements, were for the lawful purposes of said company, and the benefit of its corporators given, granted, authorized and secured to the said company and to the president and directors respectively, as fully and perfectly as if the same were herein repeated; provided, that" it shall not be lawful for the said Maryland and New York Iron and Coal Company to occupy or use any portion of the lands that may be necessary for the accommodation of the canal and works of the Chesapeake and Ohio Canal Company, or for the main route of the Baltimore and Ohio Rail Road, or that may be within the limits of either of the public roads there now existing, except to cross these roads without injury to the same; and provided also, that full right and privilege is hereby reserved to the citizens of this State, or any company now or hereafter to be incorporated under the authority of this State, to connect with the rail road hereby provided for, or any other rail road, if in the opinion and judgment of the commissioners of Allegany county, for the time being, passed upon hearing of all parties interested, no injury would be done by such connection to the rail road of said company, and that the said company shall transport on the said rail road at the rate of one cent a ton per mile on all goods, merchandise or property of any description whatsoever transported on said rail road, or on any lateral way which they may construct, and also not exceeding two cents per mile for each passenger transported on said road; provided always, that when any car shall be placed on said rail road it be adopted in size, and all necessary particulars to said rail road; and provided further, that the Legislature of this State may at any time hereafter regulate, modify or change the control, use, and estate of said rail road as shall be constructed under the authority hereby given, in such manner as it may deem equitable towards the said company, and necessary to the accommodation of the public travel or use of the said rail road."

Later, in 1841, the Charter was amended:

"Be it enacted by the General Assembly of Maryland, That it shall be lawful for the Maryland and New York Iron and Coal Company, to charge, demand and receive, for all persons and property transported on the rail road and any lateral way, which they are authorized to construct from their mines to the basin of the Chesapeake and Ohio Canal, or other points, in or near the town of Cumberland, the same rates of toll, or prices of transportation as the Baltimore and Ohio Rail Road are, or shall be, by law allowed to charge and receive. And whereas, doubts may exist whether the said company would be authorized, under the act to which this is a supplement, to construct a rail road from their mines or Works, to some intermediate point or points between the basin of the Chesapeake and Ohio Canal at Cumberland and their works or mines aforesaid, should circumstances render the extension of their road to the basin of the canal at Cumberland unnecessary, as will probably be the case, if the Baltimore and Ohio rail road company, or the said canal company, extend

63

their works up the valley of Jennings' run, to give additional facilities to the coal and iron trade—therefore,"

"Be it further enacted, That it shall not be necessary for the said Maryland and New York Iron and Coal Company, to construct their said rail road or any lateral way from their said works or mines to the basin of the said canal at Cumberland, but that the same may be stopped at any intermediate point, at the discretion of the company, and that it shall be lawful to charge the same rates of toll for the transportation of persons and property upon such road when constructed, as are authorized by the first section hereof; provided, that the said rail road be constructed so as to intersect with the extension of the Baltimore and Ohio rail road, or the Chesapeake and Ohio canal, or the improved navigation of Wills' creek, by canal or otherwise."

"And be it further enacted, That a quorum for the transaction of business of the said Maryland and New York Iron and Coal Company, shall hereafter consist of the President and any two Directors, as required by the fourth section of the act to which this is a supplement "

The Mount Savage rolling mill was built in 1843 by the Company, but it was not the path to financial success that they hoped. The company had to borrow $30,000 from Mr. Semmes, but that was only a short-term proposition. In 1848, the company failed, partially because Congress had decided to lift protective tariffs on British rail. Its property was sold at auction to John M. Forbes of Boston, who conveyed it to the Lulworth Iron Company, which had been incorporated in 1846.

Lulworth Iron Company (1847-1848)

The Lulworth Iron Company was chartered in the state of Maryland on March 1, 1847. The key players were Samuel M. Semmes, John G. Lynn, Henry Thomas Weld, Jonathan Guest, and Robert Samuel Palmer. They were empowered for "...carrying on the manufacturing of iron, and of articles of which iron is a component part, and for opening, working, transporting to market and vending the products of their lands, mines, manufactories..."

64

The charter continues, "That for the purpose of enabling said corporation to transport the produce of its mines and manufactories to market and elsewhere, in the cheapest and most expeditious manner, the said corporation and the president and directors thereof, shall be, and are respectively invested with all and singular the rights, profits, powers, privileges, authorities, immunities and advantages for the surveying, locating, establishing and constructing a rail road or rail roads, with the necessary appurtenances, beginning the same at or near the mines or manufactories of the said corporation, and running to a convenient point or points at or near the town of Cumberland, or to such other point or points as may best suit the convenience and interest of said corporation, and for the using, preserving and controlling the said rail road or rail roads, and the necessary vehicles and appurtenances thereto belonging, and every part thereof, which by the act, and more particularly the fifteenth section thereof, incorporating the Baltimore and Ohio Rail Road Company and its several supplements, were for the lawful purposes of said company, and the benefit of its corporators given, granted, authorized and secured to the said company, and to the president and directors respectively, as fully and perfectly as if the same were herein repeated; provided, that it shall not be lawful for the said Lulworth Iron Company to occupy or use any portion of the lands that may be necessary for the accommodation of the canal and works of the Chesapeake and Ohio Canal Company, or for the main route of the Baltimore and Ohio Rail Road, or that may be within the limits of either of the public roads there now existing, except to cross these roads without injury to the same; and provided also, that full right and privilege is hereby reserved to the citizens of this State, or any company now or hereafter to be incorporated under the authority of this State, to connect with the rail road or rail roads hereby provided for, or any other rail road, if in the opinion and judgment of the commissioners of Allegany county, for the time being, passed upon hearing of all parties interested, no injury would be done by such connection, to the rail road of said corporation; and that the said corporation shall transport on its said rail road or rail roads, all persons and properly, at the same rates of toll and prices of transportation as the Baltimore and Ohio Rail Road Company are, or shall be, by law, allowed to charge and receive; provided however, that in all cases where a connection is formed between the rail road or rail roads hereby authorized to be constructed, and the rail road or rail roads of any other corporation or citizen of this State, the cars to be used in the transportation of persons and property shall be adapted in size and all necessary particulars to the rail road or rail roads of the said Lulworth Iron Company; and provided further, that the Legislature of this State may at any time hereafter regulate, modify or change the control, use and estate of the rail road or rail roads to be constructed under the authority hereby given, in such manner as it may deem equitable towards the said corporation, and necessary to the accommodation of the public travel or use of the said rail road or rail roads."

In the early deeds and records the community around the furnaces was called Lulworth because the Lulworth Iron Company once owned the clay and manufacturing rights. But later the name Mount Savage appeared when it was sold again, taking its name from the one the people living in the area preferred. As a matter of record, however, the community that was slowly growing up around the brick yard, blast furnaces and railroads, was called "Savage Mountain Hamlet", but as the town grew larger, the Hamlet was dropped and "Savage Mount" continued in use for many years. Whether the "Mount Savage" had a more lyrical sound than "Savage Mount" is not known, but it became reversed and ever since was called Mount Savage. Lulworth Iron later changed its name to Mount Savage Iron Company on Feb. 7, 1848.

Mount Savage Iron Company (1848-1867)

A major investor in Mount Savage Iron was Erasmus Corning, of New York. He made John F. Winslow the President of the Company. The Mount Savage Rail Road had been built with "Winslow's Patent Rail." This was a British patent.

John A. Graham (the first president of the Cumberland & Pennsylvania Railroad) with fellow directors John F. Winslow, Warren Delano, John M. Forbes, and Joseph B. Varnum ran the company.

Lulworth Iron was essentially split into two parts. The railroad went to the C & P, and the iron manufacturing went to Mount Savage Iron. The two companies shared directors.

Mount Savage Iron did not pay cash for the shares; rather, it conveyed its existing railroad operations, stretching from the B&O depot in Cumberland and the Potomac Wharf to the mines near Frostburg, to the newly formed C & P Railroad. Thus, Mount Savage Iron was out of the railroad business directly, and the C & P was in. Mount Savage Iron completed the Canal Wharf (ex-Lynn Wharf) in Cumberland in 1850. Canal boats were loaded in the Potomac, then entered the canal via the guard locks. Mount Savage Iron operated the Mount Savage Rail Road until 1854, when it went under C & P control.

New York Mining Company (1845)

The New York Mining Company was chartered in the State of Maryland in February 26, 1845. The incorporators were Oroondates Mauran, Barrett Ames, Robert B. Minturn, Jonathan Sturges, Charles Dennison, and Samuel M. Semmes. It was allowed to mine coal and iron, and manufacture and sell iron products. Mr. Mauran was a wealthy New York businessman, who with his partner Cornelius Vanderbilt, owned the Staten Island Ferry. Robert Bowne Minturn was one of the most prominent American merchants and shippers of the mid-19th century. Today, he is probably best known as being one of the owners of the famous Clipper Ship, the Flying Cloud. He was a New York merchant, involved in the China and transatlantic trade. He and his wife donated the land for New York's Central Park.

Mount Savage Fire Brick Company (1841-present)

The Mount Savage Brick Works established its first plant in 1841. The bricks were shipped all over the country. The Mount Savage Firebrick Co., now located now in Zihlman, is still in operation.

Union Mining Company (1864-1944)

In 1864 the Union Mining Company of Allegany County was incorporated, taking over operations of the Mount Savage Fire Brick Works. The company actually dates back to 1831, when the founders had obtained a land grant in Mount Savage. A company was organized in 1837 to produce iron ore. One of the largest stockholders was the United States government. The early fire brick was imported from England, but by 1839, the requisite clay was found in Mount Savage. By 1864, the company was the largest manufacturer of fire brick in the United States. As early as 1847, the company owned 8000 acres of valuable and coal lands and employed 1100 men. It had produced the first fire brick in the United States.

The organizers of the company were George McCulloh of Frostburg, F. A. Mason, Thomas H. Frost, C. M. Graham, and John Neff. McCulloh was born in 1812, and served in the Maryland House of Delegates for Allegany County. He also served as the postmaster of Frostburg, and moved to Pittsburg around 1979. John Neff was also a Delegate from Allegany County, around 1838.

Mount Savage Enamel Brick Company (1896-1928)

The Mount Savage enamel Brick Company was founded by Andrew Ramsay, with local men John Sheridan, J. Findlay, H, McMullen, and W. Delano. At one time, the works employed 50 men. Ramsay invented a process for applying glaze to bricks in a single firing process, a secret that he took to his grave. These bricks, which came in various shapes and colors, were considered the finest and most durable in the country. They were shipped all over the Western Hemisphere. The bricks can be seen in numerous houses in Mount Savage, and buildings in Cumberland. They found use in chimney linings, and subway tunnels.

To support his reportedly lavish life style, Ramsay expanded the business into other areas. Ramsay's big mistake may have been making bathroom fixtures in competition with established manufacturers Crane, American Standard, and Koehler. While his glazed clay product was cheaper than vitreous china, it was also heavier to handle and more likely to crack or chip.

Cumberland & Pennsylvania Railroad

March 13, 1850, marked the date of incorporation of the Cumberland & Pennsylvania Railroad Company, as approved by the legislature of the State of Maryland. In 1887, The C&P filed a charter in the State of West Virginia. The Commissioners in Maryland were Robert Garrett, John Q. Hewlett, P.H. Sullivan, all of Baltimore, and William Price and George A. Thruston, of Cumberland, and Andrew Stewart and Edward D. Gayzan of Pennsylvania.

"That the President and Directors of said Company shall be, and they are hereby invested with all the rights and powers necessary to the construction and repair of a Railroad from the town of Cumberland, to some suitable point on the dividing line between the States of Maryland and Pennsylvania, to be by them determined, not exceeding sixty feet wide, with as many sets of tracks as the said President and Directors, or a majority of them, may necessary, and they, or a majority of them may cause to be made, or contract with others for making said Railroad, or any part of it, and they, their agents, or those with whom they may contract for making any part of the same, or their agents, may enter upon, and use and excavate, all lands which may be wanted for the site of said road, or the erection of warehouses or other works necessary to said road, or for any other purpose necessary or useful in the construction or repair of said road or its works, and that they may build bridges, may fix scales and weights, may lay rails, may take and use any earth, timber, gravel, stone or other materials which may be wanted for the construction or repair of any part of said road, or any of its works, and may make and construct all works whatsoever which may be necessary and expedient, in order to the proper completion of said road, and that they, or a majority of them, may make or cause to be made, lateral Railroads in any direction whatsoever, in connecting said Railroad from the town of Cumberland to the dividing line between the States of Maryland and Pennsylvania, and in the construction of the same or their works, shall have, possess, and may exercise all the rights and powers hereby given to them, in order to the construction or repair of the said Railroad, from the town of Cumberland to the dividing line between the States of Maryland and Pennsylvania."

The transportation rates were spelled out and fixed:

"..and they shall have power to charge for toll upon (and the transportation of persons) goods, produce, merchandise, or property of any kind whatsoever, transported by them along said railroad, from the town of Cumberland to the dividing line between the States of Maryland and Pennsylvania, any sum not exceeding the following rates, namely on all goods, produce, merchandise or property of any description whatsoever transported by them, not exceeding three cents a ton per mile for tolls, and three cents a ton per mile for transportation, and for the transportation of passengers, not exceeding three cents per mile for each passenger; and it shall not be lawful for any other company, or any person or persons whatsoever, to travel upon or use any of the roads of said company, or to transport persons, merchandise, produce or property of any description whatsoever, along said roads or any of them, without the license or permission of the President and Directors of said company"

Later, 4 more commissioners, all from Baltimore, were named: "James M. Buchanan, Elijah M. Bartholow, David Stewart and Charles R. Clark." In February 1866.

"And be it further enacted, That the President and Directors of said company shall be, and they are hereby invested with full right and power to connect with any existing railroad leading from the town of Cumberland at any point west of Cumberland, and to construct a railroad from the place of such connection to the Pennsylvania line, or to purchase any such railroad, or any part thereof, and the lands, franchises and appurtenances held for the purpose of the same, with power to construct and build a connection from any railroad, or part of any railroad so purchased, from any point thereof, west of Cumberland, the said President and Directors may choose, to the Pennsylvania line."

And, in fact, they had to.

"And be it further enacted, That in case said President and Directors shall purchase any existing railroad, or part of such road as aforesaid, or in case they shall make any connection With any existing railroad, and construct such connection to the Pennsylvania line as aforesaid, then so much of said Act, being the twentieth section thereof, as declares such charter forfeited, in case the road provided for in the twelfth section thereof is not commenced in six years after the passage of said Act, and shall not be completed in twelve years from the commencement thereof, shall be inoperative and void."

But this was subsequently repealed:

"And it be enacted, That the said Cumberland and Pennsylvania Railroad Company, be, and it is hereby wholly relieved from any obligation to construct a railroad to the Pennsylvania line, and that the twentieth section of said original act imposing a forfeiture in relation thereto, be and the same is hereby repealed."

And they didn't necessarily have first choice:

"Provided, that the Pittsburgh and Connellsville Rail Road Company, as proposed to be chartered, by a bill now pending, in the laying out and constructing their road from the town of Cumberland to the Pennsylvania line, shall have priority of choice over any road to be laid out or constructed by the said Cumberland and Pennsylvania Rail Road Company in the right of way."

By construction and acquisition, the C&P built itself into a formidable position, as noted by the Assembly in 1906:

"Whereas, The tracks of the said Cumberland and Pennsylvania Railroad Company now extend from Cumberland, in Allegany county, Maryland, to Piedmont, in the State of West Virginia, running through the entire coal basin of said Allegany county, and to a very large extent controlling the entire output of coal in this State."

The Assembly also noted:

"It is now apparent that the extensive corporate rights and franchises granted by this State to the said Cumberland and Pennsylvania Railroad Company are not now being used and exercised for the purpose intended by the State, but on the other hand are being used to the detriment of the material interests of the State and in such a way as to promote the development of coal fields in the State of Pennsylvania and West Virginia to the disadvantage of the State of Maryland."

The Raw Materials

The Mount Savage area has a unique combination of plentiful coal, limestone, iron ore, and fire clay, the ideal basis for a 19th century industrial base. Nothing is more than a mile or so away. Given iron ore, limestone, coal, and fire clay for a furnace lining, you can make pig iron.

Pig iron is the intermediate product of smelting iron ore with coke using limestone as a flux. Pig iron has a very high carbon content, typically 3.5–4.5% which makes it very brittle and not useful directly as a material except for limited applications.

The traditional shape of the molds used for these ingots was a branching structure formed in sand, with many individual ingots at right angles to a central channel or runner. Such a configuration is similar in appearance to a litter of piglets suckling on a sow. When the metal had cooled and hardened, the smaller ingots (the pigs) were simply broken from the much thinner runner (the sow), hence the name pig iron. As pig iron is intended for remelting, the uneven size of the ingots and inclusion of small amounts of sand was insignificant compared to the ease of casting and of handling.

Pig iron is melted and a strong current of air is directed over it while it is being stirred or agitated. This causes the dissolved impurities (such as silicon) to be thoroughly oxidized. The metal is then cast into molds or used in other processes. A puddling furnace, fired by coke or by the gas from coke production can produce wrought iron, which can be made into sheets or bars. The bars can be rolled into rails. The sheet can be curved and riveted into boilers.

Wrought iron is commercially pure iron. In contrast to steel, it has a very low carbon content. It is a fibrous material due to the slag inclusions (a normal constituent). This is also what gives it a "grain" resembling wood, which is visible when it is etched or bent to the point of failure. Wrought iron is tough, malleable, ductile, and strong in tension. Examples of items that used to be produced from wrought iron include: rivets, chains, railway couplings, water and steam pipes, raw material for manufacturing of steel, nuts, bolts, horseshoes, handrails, straps for timber roof trusses, boiler tubes, and ornamental ironwork. These are all pieces that can be used to make a locomotive.

Steel differs from iron in the carbon content, which must be carefully controlled. Steel is an alloy of iron with a carbon content between 0.2% and 2.14%. The Bessemer converter in the mid-19th century lead to the mass production of steel. The Mount Savage Works were within a year or two of making steel, before Bessemer got his process working in 1858. The first Bessemer steel mill in the United States was established in 1855 in Wyandotte, Michigan, about 14 miles south of Detroit.

But an alternative to the Bessemer is the open hearth furnace process, using the Siemens Regenerative furnace that Mount Savage is known to have had. A temperature of 1600 degrees F is required to be sustained. A Siemens furnace was first used for steel production in France is 1865.

What if? What if Mount Savage had produced the first economical steel in the United States? Would Pittsburgh still have developed as the steel-making capitol of the United States?

Fire Clay

Fire clay is a specific kind of clay used in the manufacture of ceramics, especially fire brick. The material is named for its refractory characteristics. Fire clay was discovered in the Pottsville formation near Mount Savage in 1837.

Products made from fire clay are resistant to high temperatures, have a fusion point higher than 1,600°C, and therefore are suitable for lining furnaces, as fire brick, and manufacture of utensils used in the metalworking industries, such as crucibles and glassware. Because of its stability during firing in the kiln, it can be used to make complex items of pottery such as pipes and sanitary ware. Its chemical composition consists of a high percentage of silicon and aluminum oxides, and a low percentage of the oxides of sodium, potassium, and calcium. Unlike conventional brick-making clay, fire clay is mined at depth, usually found underneath a coal seam. The formations in Allegany County range from 5 to 20 feet thick.

Iron Ore

Captain John Smith is generally credited with the discovery of iron ore in Maryland in 1608. There is no evidence that the Native American population ever smelted ore, although they did use it as a pigment. George Washington's father was involved in the early colonial period iron industry. The iron ore in the vicinity of Mount Savage had a particularly useful yield.

Coal

Bituminous coal is abundant in the Mount Savage region, as part of the Big Vein formation. Coke is better for iron making, being more pure carbon with fewer impurities. The pioneering use of coke for iron making was the furnace at Lonaconing. Previously, charcoal was used, leading to a massive destruction of trees to feed the iron furnaces.

Coke is produced by destructive distillation of low-ash, low-sulfur bituminous coal. In the very simplest case, trenches are filled with coal, set on fire, and then covered with dirt. A more sophisticated process involves baking the coal in a sealed furnace. The volatile gas given off can be useful as well.

Volatile constituents of the coal, including water, coal-gas, and coal-tar, are driven off by baking in an airless furnace or oven at temperatures as high as 2,000 degrees C. This fuses together the fixed carbon and residual ash. Most cokes in modern facilities are produced in "by-product" coking ovens and the resultant cokes are used as the main fuel in iron-making blast furnaces.

Limestone

Limestone is used in the iron making process as a flux, a material that traps contaminants. In essence, iron ore is rust. If we remove the bonded oxygen from the iron oxide, we get the pure iron back. That's the job of the carbon monoxide, produced from the burning coke. This is facilitated by high temperature. Thus, in the furnace, the iron ore is not melted – the oxygen is grabbed from it by the carbon. The free iron then melts and flows. The slag is removed from the furnace, broken up, and used for railroad ballast and fill – nothing is wasted.

The limestone also absorbs impurities from the raw iron, materials such as silicates, sulfur, and phosphorus. The mountains around Mount Savage have large amounts of limestone rock.

Captains of Industry

This section discusses some of the movers and shakers, the enablers and the technology experts who came together to make Mount Savage Industry happen.

Samuel Middleton Semmes

Semmes was born in Charles County, Maryland, in 1811. His brother Raphael went on to become an Admiral in the Confederate States Navy. Samuel graduated from Georgetown Law, and was admitted to the bar in Allegany County. He drafted most of the charters of the pioneering coal companies in Allegany County. He served as State Senator from 1855 to 1866. He was associated with Lulworth Iron, and the New York Mining Company. Semmes died in 1867.

John Galloway Lynn

The Lynn's were an 18th century Maryland family. J. G. Lynn's Father had moved to Cumberland, building a substantial brick house on the West Side known as Rose Hill. John Galloway became a Cumberland businessman, and built the Lynn Wharf along the Potomac River. This was sold by his heirs to the Maryland Mining Company. In 1849, Lynn and the Mount Savage Rail Road incorporated the Cumberland and Pittsburg (sic) Rail Road Company. Their eyes were on the grade over the Alleghenies, but nothing seems to have come of the venture.

Henry Thomas Weld

Weld was an English immigrant. The Weld's Lulworth Estate is located in central south Dorset, England. Its most notable landscape feature include a five mile stretch of coastline on the Jurassic coast. Part of the area is a special World Heritage Site. The estate is predominantly owned by the Weld family who have lived there for several generations. The Lulworth estate was once part of a grand estate under Thomas Howard, 3rd Viscount Howard of Bindon. The historic estate, of which the stately Lulworth Castle is part, was the residence to the Weld family until 1929 when it was ravaged by fire.

Henry was associated with Welds Boatyard in Cumberland, later the Weld & Sheridan Boat Building & Repair Yard at the C&O Canal basin. Captain John Sheridan was mentioned in conjunction with the Union Army in 1864, as Assistant Quartermaster at Steubenville, Ohio.

Warren Delano

Warren Delano II was the maternal grandfather of President Franklin Delano Roosevelt.. During a period of twelve years in China, Delano made more than a million dollars in the tea trade in Macau, Canton and Hong Kong, but upon returning to the United States, he lost it all in the Panic of 1857. In 1860, he returned to China and made a fortune in the controversial but highly profitable opium trade, supplying opium-based medication to the U. S. War Department during the Civil War. The Delano Mining Company operated in Mount Savage, producing coal. His partner was James Roosevelt around 1870.

The future President spend some summers with his grandfather, who lived in the Bruce estate. Delano was a director of Consolidation coal 1864-1875, and a Director of the C & P Railroad. He had a C & P locomotive named after him. This was a Winans Camel engine, acquired in 1859.

Andrew Ramsay

Andrew Ramsay was born in Scotland in 1870, and apprenticed at a brick plant, also picking up pottery and enameling skills. He came to America in 1895, and became associated with Warren Delano of New York. He took over brick manufacturing in Mount Savage, and patented and introduced a method for making enameled brick. He eventually had a branch plant in Ellerslie, Maryland, where a clay mine was also located. He formed the Andrew Ramsay Corporation in 1910, which became the Vitrox Company. He died in Ohio in 1932.

For his bride, he bought a large mansion above the brick plant, patterned after Craig Castle in Scotland. The "Castle" had been built around 1870 by a Mr. Thompson. Ramsay did various improvements and additions, using skilled workmen from his brick works. This stately Victorian home is still standing, and operates as a Bed & Breakfast.

John M. Forbes (1813-1898)

As with Jay Gould and E. H. Harriman, John Murray Forbes of Boston was an important figure in the building of America's railroad system. From March 28, 1846 through 1855, he was president of the Michigan Central Railroad, and was a Director and President of the Chicago, Burlington and Quincy Railroad. He spawned a vast 19th century Industrial Empire, starting early in the century in the China Opium trade. He and his partner Erasmus Corning of Albany bought the Mount Savage Iron works for $200,000, which was about one fifth of its value. The facility had gotten into cash flow problems, and this was the kind of deal Corning looked for. He and Forbes added the rolling mill that produced the first successful iron rail in America. The "Forbes Group" went on to acquire railroads all across America.

In *Letters and Social Aims*, Ralph Waldo Emerson said of Forbes: "Never was such force, good meaning, good sense, good action, combined with such domestic lovely behavior, such modesty and persistent preference for others. Wherever he moved he was the benefactor. How little this man suspects, with his sympathy for men and his respect for lettered and scientific people, that he is not likely, in any company, to meet a man superior to himself," and "I think this is a good country that can bear such a creature as he." (Forbes' son married Emerson's daughter).

John F. Winslow

Winslow was a partner of Erasmus Corning, and worked at the Albany and the Rensselaer Iron Works in New York in 1837. He was an engineer, ironmaster, the inventor of compound rail, and President of the Mount Savage Iron Company in 1848. He traveled extensively in Europe in 1852, buying the rights to iron and steel processes. In 1861, he partnered with John Ericson on his Navy contract to build an iron clad war ship, the *Monitor*. Some of the techniques he developed for making hardened iron plate probably came from his work at Mount Savage in the period 1848-1852.

Besides a British patent for rail, Winslow held several American patents, including number 35407, 1862, for "Improved Armor Plate for Vessels," number 34177, 1862, for "Compressing Puddle Balls," and number 4526 of 1846 for "Malleable Iron from Ores." This latter was when he worked for Corning in Troy, NY. He was also a Director of the Cumberland & Pennsylvania Railroad.

A.H. Stump - no information known

William Borden

He was president of the Borden Mining Co., circa 1875. The Borden Family was from New York. They had founded the industrial town of Fall River, Massachusetts, outside of Boston.

Enoch Pratt (1808-1896)

Capitalist, friend of Andrew Carnegie. He was born in Massachusetts, and learned ironmaking. He arrived in Baltimore in 1831 with $150, and went on to make his fortune. E. Pratt & Brothers (Hardware), 23-25 S. Charles St., Baltimore. Maryland, Steamboat Co., Director, Susquehanna Canal Co., 27 years. Vice-President of Philadelphia, Wilmington, & Baltimore Railroad, director of three other Railroads. He built and donated a public library system to the City of Baltimore.

M. B. Bramhall

Bramhall, of New York, was President of the American Coal Company.

Albert C. Green

Green was a Director of C&O Canal Co., and an outspoken superintendent of the Borden Mining Co. He was involved in canal boat construction, and mentioned as an Allegany County Commissioner in 1878.

J. B. Varnum of New York was a director of the C & P Railroad. He built the Varnum House in Mount Savage, a hotel and commercial site. It had 55 rooms, a ballroom, and commercial space including Doctor's Offices on the first floor. According to Mrs. Deffenbaugh, "it was the hotel where many an aristocrat, blacksmith, boilermaker, and machinist stayed when the C. & P. Railroad Shops built their engines." It was torn down in 1924.

John A. Graham of New York was the first President and a Director of the C & P Railroad.

Blue Collar Labor

Many Irish, Welsh and English came here to work in the rolling mills, brickyard, coal mines, and the railroad. The skilled ironworkers came from Wales, and the Irish were mostly common laborers. Competition for labor came from the railroad and canal construction projects.

The town was a cultural melting pot attracting English businessmen and Irish, Scottish, Welsh, Italian, and German workers.

The Mount Savage Iron Works built 280 company houses for their workers in 1847.

The C & P Railroad shops employed 250 to 600 men, and another several hundred were busy at the fire brick works. The railroad operating crews were the best paid in the region. In 1880, Engineers got $3.50 per day, conductors $2.50, firemen $2.10, and brakemen $1.95. Boilermakers in the shops got $2.10 a day.

A skilled worker, in 1880, earned $2.00 for a day's work of 12 hours in the winter and 10 hours in the summer. He had to work six days a week with only Sundays and Christmas day off. An ordinary laborer earned $1.25 for a single day's work.

The brickyard was lucky to get one John Davis, a Welsh former rolling mill worker. He was of tremendous height and strength. His job was to straighten the crooked rails with a 100 pound mall. He was the only man who could lift and swing it. The mall is still at the brickyard and it is referred to as "The John Davis". Davis is Mount Savage's "John Henry."

Getting the Raw Materials

The raw materials required for the production of iron includes iron ore, limestone, refractory clay, and coal, transformed to coke.

Coal mining

Coal was used from the local mines which gave rise to a long period of prosperity in manufacturing bricks, mining coal, and building engines and cars at the railroad shops. Clay was shipped to other manufacturing towns that made cement, lime pottery and enamel ware. When the brick building beside the railroad tracks was built in 1881 the lumber came from the dismantled Philadelphia Exposition.

Coke Production

Coke is made by burning coal in a closed atmosphere, which drives off the impurities, and makes the product more pure carbon. It is a destructive distillation process. Impurities such as sulfur will interfere with the purity of the iron produced, essentially poisoning the batch. What is driven off from the process is water and coal gas. The coal gas can be captured and used. At Mount Savage, it was used for the reheating furnaces. It can also provide municipal gas for cooking and lighting, In addition, passing steam or just air over hot coke produces a very clean gas product.

In 1849, coke was produced on a ledge dug out of the hill, on a level with the top of the iron furnace. The iron furnaces were loaded, or "charged" from the top. These were the first production coke ovens in Maryland. There were 28 of them, said to be smaller than the Connellsville (PA) ovens. At Mount Savage, the coke was taken out at "white heat" drenched with water, and left to cool. Coke ovens can reach 2000 degrees Celsius. The process takes a few days.

Coke is less dense than coal, thus easier to transport. Alternately, coke cars for railroad use can be larger than coal cars, without exceeding weight limits.

Limestone mining

Limestone is not really mined, but quarried. There are many exposed outcroppings of the rock in Western Maryland. It does need to be crushed into smaller pieces. It can then be burned to lime for cement, or for use as a flux for the furnaces. The *Coal Measures* limestone is used for fluxing iron.

Limestone for Mount Savage furnaces was obtained from the Dunkart Formation, some 2 miles South-East of Frostburg, and from near Corriganville, where the limestone is some 30 feet thick. In fact, the Devil's Backbone formation at the north-west side of the Narrows, with its nearly vertical strata, is limestone. There are also limestone foundations near Barrellville.

Clay Mining

Mining of Fire clay in Mount Savage began in 1839, and continues to this day. It was also brought from mines on Big Savage Mountain west of Frostburg.

Originally mined in 1839, the local product was substituted for the British product. It became a sideline for the Maryland and New York Iron & Coal Company, but a very necessary one.

The Mount Savage mines were some 2 ½ miles west of the town. The clay bed was from 8-14 feet thick, with a thin layer of coal on top. It contained both hard and soft clay.

By 1864, the Mount Savage fireclay became the standard for such in the United States.

In 1914, fire clay was mined by the Union Mining Company, Savage Mountain Firebrick Company, Big Savage Mountain Fire Brick company, and the Andrew Ramsay Company.

In 1914, The Union Mining Company's four fire clay mines were located 4 miles west of Mount Savage, on Savage Mountain. S. J. Aldon was the Superintendent, with Joseph Jenkins as the Mine Foreman. The mine cars of clay were hauled to the surface by mules and dumped into larger cars that went down a long plane by gravity. The loaded cars going down the plane hauled the empty cars back up. At the bottom of the plane, a small ('dinky") locomotive hauled the cars two miles to the Mount Savage yards. In the year of 1914, these mines employed 54 men, and produced over 33,000 tons of fire clay.

The Savage Mountain Fire brick Company had a similar operation, but used horses in place of the locomotive. The clay goes by wagon to Frostburg. Production was 10,780 tons in 1914.

The Big Savage Fire Brick Company used mules inside the mine, and a stationary engine to bring the cars a distance of 2 ½ miles to the brick yards at Allegany, on the Cumberland & Pennsylvania Railroad. They produced 11,880 tons per year.

The Ramsay Corporation Maryland Mine near Ellerslie was not used much in 1914. Three men accounted for 987 tons for the year.

The Mount Savage Refractory is still operating under the auspices of Mr. A. J. Rost of Pittsburgh, who had purchased the assets of the Union Mining

Company in 1944. This makes the Mount Savage facility the oldest firebrick plant in the United States.

There are two major types of fireclay used in the production of bricks. Flint clay, or hard clay, exhibits little or no shrinkage when fired. Plastic, or soft clay absorbs water and is easily workable. The correct mixture is critical. Both types consist of silica and alumina, in different proportions. The deposits available to Mount Savage include both types of clay. Serendipitously, the fireclay is found with seams of coal.

Iron Mining

The iron ore around Mount Savage is carboniferous and from the Clinton Ores, which are hematite.

Iron manufacturing in Mount Savage

Many Irish, Welsh and English came to Mount Savage to work in the rolling mills, brickyard, coal mines, and the railroad. The skilled iron workers came from Wales, and the Irish were mostly common laborers. Competition for labor came from the railroad and canal construction projects. The town was a cultural melting pot attracting English businessmen and Irish, Scottish, Welsh, Italian, and German workers. The Mount Savage Iron Works built 280 company houses for their workers in 1847.

The C & P Railroad shops employed 250 to 600 men, and another several hundred were busy at the fire brick works. The railroad operating crews were the best paid in the region. In 1880, Engineers got $3.50 per day, conductors $2.50, firemen $2.10, and brakemen $1.95. Boilermakers in the shops got $2.10 a day.

A skilled worker, in 1880, earned $2.00 for a day's work of 12 hours in the winter and 10 hours in the summer. He had to work six days a week with only Sundays and Christmas day off. An ordinary laborer earned $1.25 for a single day's work.

The brickyard was lucky to get one John Davis, a Welsh former rolling mill worker. He was of tremendous height and strength. His job was to straighten the crooked rails with a 100 pound mall. He was the only man who could lift and swing it. The mall is still at the brickyard and it is referred to as "The John Davis". Davis is Mount Savage's "John Henry."

The Iron furnace at Lonaconing

The precursor of the iron furnaces at Mount Savage was the furnace at Lonaconing, located some 13 miles away in the Georges Creek Valley. The furnace at Lonaconing (still extant) was a model for the ones at Mount Savage, and there was technology sharing, if not industrial espionage. See the discussion in the Lonaconing section of this book.

Mount Savage Blast Furnaces

The blast furnace process of producing iron requires a ready source of iron ore, limestone, a fuel, and a blast. The preferred fuel is coke, nearly pure carbon, made from coal. The preferred blast is heated air. The limestone serves as a flux, to collect the impurities from the ore. Iron ore was mined locally, and limestone came from nearby quarries, perhaps at Corrigansville. Coal was burned into coke onsite in long pits. This removed the sulfur and phosphorous, which interfered with the iron extraction process. The process of extracting iron from ore is less of a melting process than a chemical reduction process. The carbon from the coke binds with the oxygen from the iron oxides in the ore, and goes off as carbon dioxide and carbon monoxide. Sometimes, the iron ore was also roasted before being introduced into the furnace. This served to remove contaminants present in the raw ore.

Iron ore was mined in various locations in the county, and went to the furnaces at Mount Savage. One mine that served the Mount Savage facility was on the Samuel Eckles property on the west side of Will's Mountain. This area was worked from 1845 to 1855, and re-opened during the Civil War. Iron ore was mined in the town of Mount Savage, on the north and west side. The larger mines were on the hill called Ridgeley, and about 1 1/2 miles west of town, one the north side of Dutch Hollow. At the foot of the Mount Savage gravity plane, the "Lower Tunnel" was opened in 1846, and was worked until 1853. This tunnel was reported to be 1/2 mile long. The "Upper Tunnel" was located on the property of Henry Collins, and was also about 1/2 mile long. These excavations also yielded fireclay.

Iron ore from George Jeffries & Sons of Frostburg went to Mount Savage. About 5,000 tons were provided at a cost of $4.50 to $5.00 per ton. The Jeffries paid a royalty of $.25 per ton to the Frosts, owners of the land. The ore bed was 18 inches thick, and was recovered by drift or strip mining. This mine closed about 1855. Jeffries then worked a mine during the Civil War on the Johnson property in Frostburg. This was a parcel of land 2 acres in extent, with a vein 4 feet thick. About 10,000 tons were extracted by 10 men, and numerous teams of horses. Joseph Johnson got a royalty of $.30 per ton.

Three furnaces were built at Mount Savage, but only two went into service. The two that did go into blast resembled the furnace at Lonaconing, fifty feet high, fifteen wide at the bosh, and built against the side of a hill. They were on the south side of Jennings run. The third furnace was not built against a hill, and would have had to be loaded by derrick. The furnaces were lined with firebrick, produced locally. That fireclay and firebricks became the basis of a business that continues into recent times. The Lonaconing facility produced its last batch of pig iron in 1855.

The blowing engines at Mount Savage came from the West Point Foundry in New York in 1845, as had the ones for the furnace at Lonaconing. They were sized for furnaces making 400 tons of iron per week. Then engines were of the condensing type (recycling water), with a 56-inch diameter cylinder and a 10 foot stroke. They made 15 revolutions per minute, producing steam at 60 pounds per square inch and generating 80 horsepower. The associated boilers were 60 inches in diameter and 24 feet long. The grates spanned a total of 198 square feet. The blast cylinders were massive, being 126 inches in diameter with a 10 foot stroke. They operated at 15 revolutions per minute, and supplied air at 4-5 pounds per square inch pressure. One engine was used for the blast furnaces, and the other for the rolling mill. At the time, they were the largest cast cylinders in the world.

Early experiments with a coke-fueled furnace at Mount Savage in 1842 had produced acceptable iron at a cost of $16. per ton, when English iron was available for $15.84. A tariff bill, passed by Congress in 1846, removed protective duties on imported iron products. This benefited the English and Welsh manufacturers, at the expense of the fledgling American shops. This action was a direct cause of the failure of the Maryland & New York Iron & Coal Company, owner of the facility at Mount Savage. A poor showing for the facility that was, at one time, the largest manufacturer of iron in the United States. Mount Savage, at the time, represented one of the largest and most successful technology research and development facilities in the country, if not the hemisphere.

The 1846 Walker tariff was a United States Democratic Party-passed bill that reversed the high rates of tariffs imposed by the Whig-backed "Black Tariff" of 1842 under president John Tyler. The Democratic Party is one of the two major political parties in the United States. ...A tariff (sometimes known as a customs duty) is a tax on imported or exported goods. The Tariff of 1842, or Black Tariff as it became known, was a protectionist tariff schedule adopted in the United States to reverse the effects of the Compromise Tariff of 1833.

The Walker tariff act was named after Robert J. Walker, who was formerly a Democratic Senator from Mississippi and served as Secretary of the Treasury under president James K. Polk. The tariff's reductions coincided with Britain's repeal of the Corn Laws earlier that year, leading to a decline in protection in both. The Corn Laws, in force between 1815 and 1846, were import tariffs ostensibly designed to protect British farmers and landowners, against competition from cheap foreign grain imports.

Shortly after his election President Polk asserted that the reduction of the "Black Tariff" of 1842 would constitute the first of the "four great measures" that would define his administration. This proposal was intended to be the fulfillment of his campaign pledge in the Kane Letter on tariff policy that contributed to his victory in 1844 over Henry Clay. In 1846 Polk delivered his tariff proposal, designed by Walker, to Congress. Walker urged its adoption in order to increase commerce between the United States and Britain. He also predicted that a reduction in overall tariff rates would stimulate overall trade, and with it imports. The result, asserted Walker, would be a net increase in tax revenue despite a reduction in the rates. The Tariff of 1842, or Black Tariff as it became known, was a protectionist tariff schedule adopted in the United States to reverse the effects of the Compromise Tariff of 1833. The Kane Letter was a widely circulated letter written by James K. Polk to James Kane outlining his beliefs on tariffs, free trade, and protectionism during his 1844 campaign for President of the United States.

The Democratic-controlled Congress quickly acted on Walker's recommendations. The Walker Tariff bill produced the nation's first standardized tariff by categorizing goods into distinct schedules at identified ad valorem rates rather than assigning individual taxes to imports on a case by case basis. The bill reduced rates across the board on most major import items save luxury goods such as tobacco and alcohol. An Ad valorem tax is a tax based on the assessed value of real estate or personal property. The Tarriff of 1842 placed a duty on pig iron of $9. per ton, and for manufactured iron, $25. per ton. The ad valorum tax was set at 30%. Higher tarrifs were good for the iron industry, but bad for the railroads.

The bill resulted in a moderate reduction in many tariff rates and was considered a success in that it stimulated trade and brought needed revenue into the U.S. Treasury, as well as improved relations with Britain that had soured over the Oregon boundary dispute. As Walker predicted, the new tariff stimulated revenue intake from $30 million annually under the Black Tariff in 1845 to almost $45 million annually by 1850. Exports to and imports from Britain rose rapidly in 1847 as both countries lowered their tariff barriers against each other.

The 1846 tariff rates initiated a fourteen year period of relative free trade by nineteenth century standards lasting until 1860. It was passed along with a series of financial reforms proposed by Walker..

The Walker Tariff remained in effect until the protectionism, which reduced rates further. Both were reversed in 1861 with the adoption of the Republican-backed Morrill Tariff.

Producers from other traditional protectionist constituencies such as iron, glass, and sheep farmers opposed the bill. When the Panic of 1857 struck later that year, protectionists, led by economist Henry C. Carey, blamed the downturn recession on the new Tariff schedule. Though economists today reject this explanation, Carey's arguments rejuvenated the protectionist movement and prompted renewed calls for a tariff increase. The Tariff of 1857's cuts lasted only three years. In 1861, the country changed course again under the heavily protectionist Morrill Tariff. But it was too late for Maryland & New York Iron & Coal.

In the 1850's, the blast furnaces of Mount Savage blazed around the clock, consuming massive amounts of coked coal, iron ore, scrap iron, and limestone. According to surviving records, in June of 1856, 356.5 tons of iron were produced. This required 747 tons of iron ore (at a 39 percent yield), 1.77 tons of coke per ton of iron produced, and 1.19 tons of limestone per ton. For this process, 536 tons of coal went to the blast engines. All of this raw material was dug by hand. The cost of production totaled $23.39 per ton, including anticipated repairs to the furnace, and wages. In 1844, number 2 furnace was in blast for 40 weeks, and produced 4,500 tons of iron. In 1846, number 1 furnace was in blast for 44 weeks, and produced over 4,500 tons. The integrated manufacturing center at Mount Savage, with its associated transportation infrastructure, represented the very cutting edge of the Industrial Revolution in America, and rivaled the best in the world. Economic issues, not technological ones, forced the shutting down of the blast furnaces in the late 1840's, but they were re-opened during the Civil War.

From 1840-1860, profits in the iron business ranged from 40-60 percent, sometimes reaching 100 percent. Maryland was seventh in the nation in iron production in 1860, rising to fifth by 1870. The production of iron in Maryland declined sharply after that. The Maryland ore was never that good, and the discovery of rich veins in the West put the smaller, locally furnaces out of the iron business. Ruins of two of the furnaces are still visible in the town of Mount Savage, and the Lonaconing furnace has been preserved in a city park. The Mount Savage blast furnaces had their own railroad branch, extending 1.3 miles from the main line. Bits of this roadbed can still be found

The furnace complexes at Lonaconing and Mount Savage may have been too technologically advanced for their time, according to Harvey. The Lonaconing facility had suffered from a lack of transportation. This error was not repeated at Mount Savage. However, the politics of international trade skewed the equations in favor of imported rather than home-produced iron.

Cast iron, extracted from ore, is at best an intermediate product. Cast iron is only suitable for a limited number of products. The next step in production involves another furnace and a rolling mill.

The following page shows a reproduction of what we would now call a production spreadsheet

MOUNT SAVAGE BLAST FURNACE, No. 1

STATEMENT OF WORK and COST OF IRON for *Week* ending 25 *June* 1856

Coke	used		charges a *1005* lbs. ea.		Tons	*187.60*
Limestone	"		*246* " *1680 3*			*91.30*
Ores	"		*35 3*			*278.90*
			Fossil		Tons	*161.00*
			Cross Cut			*31.30*
			South Branch			
	Roasted Cinder					*22.00*
			Clear Spring			*214.30*
			Scrap Iron			

Pig Iron made . . . . Tons *84*

Yield of above mixture of Ores *39* 7/100 per cent. or *2* 55/100 tons Ore per ton Iron

Coke	used per ton Iron	*2.23*	tons a $ *3.00*			$	*6*	*69*
Limestone	" " "	*1.08*	" a $ *.19*				—	*45*
Ores	" " "	Fossil	*1.91* tons a $ *3.00*	$ *5.73*				
		Cross Cut	*.37* " $ *3.00*	$ *1.11*				
		South Branch	" $	$				
		Cinder	*.27* " $ *.20*	$ *0.05*			*6*	*89*
		Clearspring	" $	$				
		Scrap Iron	" $	$				
			$	$				
			$	$				

Wages, per time list, inclusive of salary of Manager,

$ *331.99* divided by *84* tons . . . . *3* | *95*

96 cars Coal to Engine *146* 57/100 tons a $ *1.20* divided by *84* Tons *2* | *09*

Materials, per Store and other accounts, viz: Oil, Tallow, Hemp, Packing Yarn, Steel, Leather, Shovels, Buckets, — | *65*

Nails, &c. &c. *Expenses for Repairing damage by fire* . . . *84*

Cost of one ton Pig Iron . . . $ *21* | *96*

Original record taken from only remaining records.
All other records of the company were lost in the great
Baltimore fire.

Mt. Savage Iron Works,
185

Saml Danks Superintendent.

The Rolling Mill, and the First Iron Rail

The iron furnaces produced cast iron; at best, an intermediate product. Early rails were cast, but these were prone to fracture. Pig iron is good for some things, but a better product was needed. This section examines the next step – a value-added process to turn pig iron into motive power. A forge and rolling mill had been planned for the facility at Lonaconing, but these were never built. .

In 1842, the American Railroad Journal had said in an editorial that there was no firm in the United States capable of manufacturing heavy-edged rail. Many facilities had tried and failed to produce an acceptable product. The market for the product was apparent and the Mount Savage rolling mill was built in 1843 by the Maryland & New York Iron & Coal Company. The rolling mill site had 3 trains of rollers driven by steam engines, 17 puddling furnaces, 6 reheating furnaces, and 3 special facilities for sheet iron production. The furnaces were of the Siemens type, using coal gas produced onsite as fuel. A medal for the process was awarded in October 1844 from the Franklin Institute of Philadelphia. The medal was at one time a part of the collection of the Museum of Ince Blundell in Lancashire, England. In 1844, there was just over 4,000 miles of railroad in America.

The Mount Savage open hearth furnaces were not making true steel – just malleable iron. The difference between cast iron, wrought iron, and steel is a percentage point or two of carbon. The rival Bessemer process made steel in England by 1856. William and Frederick Siemens built their first experimental furnace in 1858, and got a patent in 1861. By 1868, they finally demonstrated the production of steel from pig iron.

The Siemens furnace was a rectangular, covered design that passed burning gas over the top of the charge of pig iron. The early models had a 4-5 ton capacity. The process was to purify the pig iron by oxidation of the carbon, and to remove impurities.

The production of coal gas is a byproduct of coke production, but in carefully designed reactors, a better grade of gas is produced. Typically, a producer reaction vessel is used, being constructed of cylindrical steel like a boiler, and lined with firebrick. It was partially filled with coal or coke. A blast of air, and sometimes steam, was introduced from the bottom. These reactors consume several tons of coal per hour.

A successful rolling mill had been placed in operation in England as early as 1783, and cold rolling began in Pittsburgh in 1860.

In addition to rolled product such as rail, the production facility could produce wrought iron sheet. Rolled into cylinders and riveted, this made the production of locomotive boilers possible. In addition, wrought iron was used in the production of chain, engine bolts, stay bolts, pipe and threaded parts, and drawbars.

The first successful output of the Mount Savage mill was in 1844, and marked the end of the U. S. dependence on imported products. Interestingly, in the same year, iron ore was discovered around Lake Superior. This would lead to the demise of Mount Savage in particular and Maryland in general, as world-class iron producers.

The 43 pounds to the yard rail was used for the home road and sold to the B&O railroad, which up to that time had been dependent on imported British rail. One thousand tons of rail, at $59 per ton, went to a railroad at Fall River, Massachusetts. Most interestingly, the Mount Savage facility used its own product to build the Mount Savage Rail Road, down the Jennings Run and through the Narrows, to connect with the B&O at Cumberland. An additional customer included the Hampshire Coal & Iron Company for their tram road near Piedmont, WV. The Utica & Schenectady and the Hudson River Railroad in New York, and the Erie and the Reading in Pennsylvania were also customers. The Utica and Schenectady ordered 1,000 tons of rail. There was a display of Mount Savage rail at the Mechanics Fair in Baltimore in November 1850. E. Pratt & Brother were the agents.

During the Civil War, the facilities at Mount Savage went back to work. Some 333 tons of railroad iron were taken by US forces in 1864 in Louisiana. The government reimbursed the company for the cost. The rail had originally been sold to the El Paso Pacific Company in Texas, but never used. Some 53 tons were lost to Confederate forces.

John W. Brown of Mount Savage was granted a patent for a T-iron rail rolling mill in April 1856. It describes a five-step process, which not only forms bar iron into rail, but controls the displacement and density of the finished shape, and the hardness of the wearing surfaces.

In the 1850's, the Mount Savage facilities employed 900. Jobs at Mount Savage attracted both skilled and unskilled immigrants from Ireland, England, and Wales. In foundries and machine shops wages were relatively stable from the early 1880's to the 1910's. A machinist or boilermaker would make about $2.50 per 10-hour day, 6 days a week, 300 days per year. There was no vacation, no sick leave, no holidays except for Christmas day. The employees were paid in script, exchangeable at the company store, until the 1880's

Pudding furnaces were making malleable iron out of pig iron in England by 1784. In these, the molten metal with a layer of floating slag is stirred for 5-10 minutes of clearing. This causes the oxidation of contaminates in the iron, mainly silicon, manganese, and phosphorous. The puddler's job was a particularly hot and dangerous one. He stirred the molten iron with a long rod, to bring the slag and impurities to the surface, where they could be skimmed off. Still, it was probably a better job than in the nearby mines. His skill was also critical. There was no way to accurately measure the temperature of the melt, except by its color. The ironmaster's calibrated eyeballs were the key to success or failure of the process.

After clearing, the temperature in the furnace was raised. After another 10 minutes of stirring, carbon monoxide gas would begin to escape the melt as bubbles, which catch fire as they burst. This phenomenon was called puddler's candles. When they disappeared, more stirring was called for. This got increasingly difficult, as globules of decarburized iron formed. These 150 pound semi-plastic balls were grasped by tongs and removed from the furnace. These were then hammered or squeezed by rollers. The resulting rough bars were cut into short pieces, and went into a reheating furnace. Here, they were taken to white heat – a self-welding temperature. They would be worked and reheated numerous times. Each reworking with a hammer or rollers removed more slag.

For the rolling operation, the worked iron was again reheated, and passed through the roll multiple times to get the correct shape. The Mount Savage rail of 1844 was a U shaped design. Rolled rail would have a natural curvature as it cooled, and would be bent to be straight. It would then be weighed for quality purposes, and stamped. Later, heat-treating of the working face would be used. Plate was also rolled in a similar process to rails. It would then be sheared to size, and holes for rivets would be punched.

The production of coal gas is a byproduct of coke production, but in carefully designed reactors, a better grade of gas is produced. Typically, a producer reaction vessel is used, being constructed of cylindrical steel like a boiler, and lined with firebrick. It was partially filled with coal or coke. A blast of air, and sometimes steam, was introduced from the bottom. These reactors consume several tons of coal per hour.

The design and construction of the rolls were critical. Templates would be constructed first of wood, then of brass. Trial rolls would be made, and iron would pass through the process. These sections were then sawed and inspected. During the rolling and forming process, the progress of the iron would be carefully watched. The rolls would wear at different rates, requiring different replacement intervals.

In addition to rolled product such as rail, the production facility could produce wrought iron sheet. Rolled into cylinders and riveted, this made the production of locomotive boilers possible. In addition, wrought iron was used in the production of chain, engine bolts, stay bolts, pipe and threaded parts, and drawbars.

The first successful output of the Mount Savage mill was in 1844, and marked the end of the U. S. dependence on imported products. Interestingly, in the same year, iron ore was discovered around Lake Superior. This would lead to the demise of Mount Savage in particular and Maryland in general, as world-class iron producers.

The 43 pounds to the yard rail was used for the home road and sold to the B&O railroad, which up to that time had been dependent on imported British rail. One thousand tons of rail, at $59 per ton, went to a railroad at Fall River, Massachusetts. Most interestingly, the Mount Savage facility used its own product to build the Mount Savage Rail Road, down the Jennings Run and through the Narrows, to connect with the B&O at Cumberland. An additional customer included the Hampshire Coal & Iron Company for their tram road near Piedmont, WV. The Utica & Schenectady and the Hudson River Railroad in New York, and the Erie and the Reading in Pennsylvania were also customers. The Utica and Schenectady Railroad ordered 1,000 tons of rail. There was a display of Mount Savage rail at the Mechanics Fair in Baltimore in November 1850. E. Pratt & Brother were the agents.

During the Civil War, the facilities at Mount Savage went back to work. Some 333 tons of railroad iron from Mount Savage were taken by US forces in 1864 in Louisiana. The government reimbursed the company for the cost. The rail had originally been sold to the El Paso Pacific Company in Texas, but never used. Some 53 tons were lost to Confederate forces.

John W. Brown of Mount Savage was granted a patent for a T-iron rail rolling mill in April 1856. It describes a five-step process, which not only forms bar iron into rail, but controlled the displacement and density of the finished shape, and the hardness of the wearing surfaces.

The firm of Manning & Lee, Charles & Towsend Streets, Baltimore, were Agents for the Mount Savage works. In 1845 and 1846, they brokered the sale of "T" rail to a Boston Purchaser. This is most likely the delivery for the Fall River, Massachusetts, railroad. Manning & Lee were also agents for the Avalon Iron Works, who later sold rail to the B&O.

Industrial safety was a concept that developed slowly and the iron shops of the 19th century were dangerous places to work. As part of the social contract men injured at work usually had guaranteed lifetime employment -- if they survived.

From 1840-1870, Maryland was seventh in the nation in iron production, rising to fifth, but iron manufacture in Maryland declined sharply after that. The Maryland ore was never that good and the discovery of rich veins in the Great Lakes Region, coupled with the emergence of the huge integrated iron conglomerates in the Pittsburgh Region and southwestern Pennsylvania, put small, local operations like that at Mount Savage out of business. The Mount Savage rolling mill closed in 1868 and was dismantled by 1875. It was cheaper to buy steel from Pittsburgh. No trace of the mill remains, but ruins of two of the blast furnaces are still visible in the town of Mount Savage, and the Lonaconing furnace has been preserved as a historic landmark.

Where many hundreds of men labored in literally hellish conditions, a stranglehold on the rail industry by British industry was broken, and the tools for industrial expansion of the United States were produced.

Brick, Fire brick, and enameled brick manufacturing

Although Mount Savage became noted for its bricks, the first bricks used there were imported from England for the blast furnaces. Fire clay was found later when geologists were exploring for ores. Although the iron ore was of inferior quality, the clay was of the finest and about the year 1839 a small building was built for making brick. The first plant was in back of the railroad depot but, after the blast furnaces and rolling mills were abandoned, the clay company moved into quarters on Calla Hill extending on down to the present locations and Mount Savage really became a brick manufacturing town. Clay was also shipped to other manufacturing towns that made cement, lime pottery and enamel ware.

The earliest bricks were molded by hand in wooden molds, and burned in kilns. Later, Union Mining introduced continuous kilns, fired by producer gas. The bricks take 5-6 days to burn, and several days to cool.

Some of the Ramsay product found its way into the construction of the Buffalo Post Office, the Boston Back Bay Train Station, and the Boston Union Station.

Locomotive manufacturing

After the civil war, James A. Millholland came down from Pennsylvania to set up the C & P shops. A period of locomotive rebuildings and experimentation followed, culminating in the production of engines at Mount Savage.

Millholland's Locomotive Shops

The C & P locomotive shops were established in Mount Savage in 1866, under the direction of James A. Millholland. The original locomotive shop was constructed of stone and was 90 feet x 250 feet in size with a 33 foot high roof. An adjoining car shop, built at about the same time, was also of stone and was later extended with a wooden structure. These buildings still stand and are in use in Mount Savage.

James Millholland, Senior, was 54 years old when he and his family came to Mount Savage from Reading, Pennsylvania. Millholland was a master mechanic and an "advocate of plain engines and simplicity." He had extensive experience in keeping Winans camel engines running from his earlier work in Pennsylvania with the Baltimore & Susquehanna and he was credited with many important locomotive innovations. He came in 1866 as the President of Consolidation Coal, and of the C & P Railroad. He resigned in 1869, retiring to his estate on the Valley Road in Cumberland. He was credited with developing the first anthracite burning locomotive, and was Superintendent of Motive Power for the line for many years. He is also credited with constructing the first iron deck girder bridge in the United States for the Baltimore & Susquehanna Railway near Bolton in 1846-47. He was responsible for so many improvements to the basic Winans camel engine, the class was referred to as "Millholland Camel's". He is credited with designing a 12-wheeled camel engine, built in the Pennsylvania & Reading shops in 1863.

His son, James A. was 24 years old when the family moved to Mount Savage. He had been born in Reading, in 1842, and had apprenticed in the railroad shops. He also joined the C & P, becoming Master Mechanic, and was vice-president by the time his father retired. He was listed as the Second Vice

President of the Georges Creek Coal & Iron Company in 1869. He left the C & P in 1879 to join the new Georges Creek & Cumberland Railroad. The younger Millholland was tasked with building the C & P shops, to maintain the mixed fleet of motive power. He had the right experience for the job.

Millholland bought quality machine tools, which were still in use 40 years later as evidenced by the 1917 ICC valuation. He equipped the shops with metal working machinery from Bement & Dougherty, probably a predecessor of Wm. B. Bement & Son of Philadelphia.

Initially, the work supervised by Millholland at the Mount Savage Shops was limited to repairing and rebuilding the Winans Camels and other early C & P locomotives. The shop force gained valuable hands-on experience during the first twenty years; at least 15 of the C & P's Camel locomotives were rebuilt at Mount Savage (some twice). Typical of the rebuilds was the engine *Highlander*, a Winans Camel inherited from the Mount Savage Rail Road. This was a modernization project in which, among other things, the cab was relocated from on top of the boiler to the rear position. The C & P shops also provided repair services to its rivals in the Georges Creek coal region.

By the 1880's, the shops that Millholland had set up apparently had built quite an extensive operation, able to offer custom built locomotives for sale in addition to meeting the requirements of the parent C & P. The period beginning in 1883 was an exciting one for heavy manufacturing in Mount Savage. A locomotive catalog listing five types of engines for sale and their specifications was issued for the Works by their agent, Thomas B. Inness & Co. of Broadway, New York.

The first recorded engine 'build' was a 0-10-0 unit in 1868. This could have been a modification to a Winans Camel. Engine production was active between 1885 and 1917. Engines were produced for other roads as well as the C & P. The production figures for 1882 list 19 passenger and freight engines outshopped, with 16 more in 1883.

A new 4-stall roundhouse was built in Mount Savage in 1898. It was reported then that the locomotive shops were working 5 hours of overtime every evening.

The following table shows some of the machinery used in the original shop. All of the rotating power machinery was driven by leather belts from overhead master shafts. These, in turn, were powered by a stationery steam engine in the adjacent power house. A similar facility may be seen today preserved at the East Broad Top Railroad, in Pennsylvania.

Mount Savage Locomotive Shops Heavy Machinery

- Engine lathe, 28" x 8 foot bed
- Horizontal boring and drilling machine, table size 24" x 44"
- 18" x 48" engine lathe, C & P
- 18" x 24" engine lathe, C & P
- vertical boring mill 54"
- car wheel boring mill, 48" table
- 10" slotter

- wooden jib crane, 20' mast, 15' boom, 4.5 ton capacity, C & P
- punch & shear, 30" throat (used for rivet holes)

Car shop

- 18" rip saw
- Lowell drill press
- Tice shaper/molder

Blacksmith shop

- Fulton 500 pound power forge hammer

One particularly good customer was T. H. Paul & Sons of Frostburg. A former C & P master mechanic himself (1854-1855), Paul established shops in Frostburg and Cumberland. He built mine engines and smaller narrow gauge locomotives at his shops, but contracted with Mount Savage for his larger orders. His Frostburg works were located near the existing C & P Passenger station on Depot Hill, and some of the buildings still stand.

A locomotive catalog was issued by Thomas B. Inness & Co. in 1883. The catalog listed five types of engines for sale, and their specifications. Evidence was that the catalog was successful, and numerous sales to other roads resulted. This helped finance production for the home road, spurred development, and helped employment. Narrow gauge engines proved so popular a product that the Mount Savage works installed a third rail up the main line from Mount Savage for customer acceptance testing of narrow-gauge equipment.

Locomotive manufacturing during this period was hard, heavy, dangerous work. It proceeded according to numerous 'rules of thumb' developed by the master mechanics over the years. Innovations were introduced slowly. There were continuous efforts to reduce costs, and increase performance. Weight reduction was not desirable, as weight-on-drivers contributed directly to tractive effort. Locomotive frames were usually riveted, built-up construction, of wrought iron and later steel.

According to White, experience at the Norris locomotive works showed that a team of 14 men could build a locomotive in 15 days. This was assuming the parts were on hand. A locomotive is a carefully integrated collection of a large number of specialty parts. The typical boiler was constructed of 5/16" wrought iron, starting as plate, and rolled to shape. The lap joints were single riveted. There is a long way between watertight and steam tight. Later, double riveting, and reinforced butt joints were used. Welding was not yet a developed technology, particularly for a pressure vessel. Boiler tubes were typically iron tubing of 2 inches diameter. They were lap welded, and reportedly difficult to flange.

The cylinders were usually cast in halves, assembled, and bored to size. This represented the most complex and expensive operation of the whole locomotive assembly. In 1856, it was common for the boring operation to consume 2 days. The pistons were cast iron, with fitted brass piston rings.

Boilers were covered, or lagged, to reduce hear loss, and increase efficiency. Wood slats were used originally. After 1900, asbestos was a favored lagging material. It was common for the slabs of the mineral to be machined to fit. This produced large clouds of asbestos dust that is now known to be a major carcinogen, a significant cause of lung cancer. The use of dust masks, hearing protection, and safety glasses was unknown at the time. The boiler shops were a haze of asbestos dust.

Millholland favored Giffard's water injectors, based on the favorable experience with them on the Reading line. He was also an early advocate of feedwater heaters, using them as early as 1855. His designs have them on the right side, under the engine running board. They are about 10 feet long, and 8" in diameter. These are a visible clue to engines produced in Mount Savage. Millholland is also responsible for the development of the poppet throttle, originally retrofitted on Camel engines in Pennsylvania.

The driving wheels were typically cast iron, and axles were usually 6" diameter wrought iron. Driving wheels were fitted with replaceable tires. On the basis of his previous experience, Millholland favored cast iron tires, shrunk onto the wheels. His father had experimented with steel tires around 1851-52, and they became standard later. Some early accidents on the C & P involved wheel failures. In 1872, Engine No. 11 broke a wheel below Frostburg, requiring the assistance of the work train, and delaying the pay car, according to the Frostburg Mining Journal.

Connecting rods were cast, and bearings were brass and/or Babbitt metal. The early lubricants were all animal fat based, and only suitable for low temperature applications. Later, petroleum based lubricants provided much better performance.

Engine safety appliances were sparse. The Bourdon Gauge for pressure readings was patented in 1849. A rival gauge was developed in 1857 by Wooten. The McKaig Company of Cumberland were producing steam pressure gauges. Glass sight gauges for boiler water level were not popular until the 1890's. Head lights were originally oil lamps. These units were box-shaped, and had a 18-22" parabolic reflector. They could cast a 1000' beam, sufficient for low-speed operation. An important improvement was introduced with the advent of lamps powered by carbide. Similar to the lamps used by miners, these lamps used the reaction of water and the mineral calcium carbide to produce acetylene gas, which burned with a bright light. Later, electric lamps and generators were fitted. C & P tenders were also fitted with lamps on the rear, since the engines frequently operated in reverse on the various coal branches where they could not easily be turned.

Engine Rebuildings at Mount Savage Shops

The following table shows the documented engine rebuildings at Mount Savage. Millholland had extensive experience with rebuilding and upgrading the Winans design. This list is derived from Hicks. It covers the major engine rebuildings for the home road, not routine maintenance or quick operational repairs. H-B refers to the manufacturer Hayward-Bartlett.

C & P Engine Rebuildings at Mount Savage

No.	Original	Date	Notes

3	Winans	1866-75	weight increase
10	Winans	1866-75	
12	Winans	1866-75	
13	Winans	1866-75	
1	Winans	12/1868	weight increase
2	Winans	6/1868	weight increase
22	Winans	1870	due to boiler explosion
23	Winans	1870	
4	Winans	1874	
31	Baldwin	1879	
5(32)	Baldwin	1885	
14	H-B	1887	
25	Baldwin	1888	
15	H-B	1888	
16	H-B	1889	
17	Norris	1898	
25	Baldwin	9/1901	2nd rebuild
17	Norris	1902	2nd rebuild
7	Baldwin	- ? -	0-6-0 -> 2-6-0
9	Winans	- ? -	
18	Norris	- ? -	0-8-0 to 0-10-0
19	Norris	- ? -	0-8-0 to 0-10-0
20	H-B	- ? -	0-8-0 to 0-10-0
21	H-B	- ? -	0-8-0 to 0-10-0
22	Winans	-?-	2nd rebuild

Repairs and rebuildings continued into the 1940's. The shops equipment was available for charitable work as well. In 1937, the Mount Savage Fire Department built their own fire truck, with the help of the railroad shops (Cumberland Times, August 8, 1937).

Engine Construction at Mount Savage for the C & P

The following table shows 31 identified engine constructions at the Mount Savage Shops for the C & P. Engine 34 was not completed, and its boiler went to the Western Maryland Railway.

No.	date	wheels	notes
24	1868	0-10-0	First engine
3	1888	2-8-0	was number 18. Sold Miller's Creek
4	1889	2-8-0	was number 20. Sold Miller's Creek
11	5/1889	2-8-0	ex-51
12	9/1889	2-8-0	ex-52
13	9/1890	2-8-0	ex-53
14	5/1891	2-8-0	ex-54
15	12/1891	2-8-0	ex-55
16	8/1892	2-8-0	ex-56
7	11/1892	2-6-0	sold to 'a steel Co. in Pa'
8	1892	2-6-0	
17	1895	2-8-0	ex 57
18	1896	2-8-0	ex-58
19	8/1897	2-8-0	ex-59, sold, Millers Creek
20	6/1898	2-8-0	ex-60
21	1899	2-8-0	
22	1899	2-8-0	ex-61
26	9/1899	2-8-0	ex-62
24	9/1901	2-8-0	
9	5/1902	4-6-0	
25	12/1902	2-8-0	
10	10/1903	4-6-0	ex-30
23	10/1904	2-8-0	ex-19
32	1910	2-8-0	
28	6/1910	2-8-0	
27	2/1910	2-8-0	
29	1912	2-8-0	
30	1913	2-8-0	
31	1915	2-8-0	
33	1917	2-8-0	Last unit
34	1917	2-8-0	not completed; boiler went to Western

Maryland

Millers Creek Railroad, in Van Lear Kentucky, was also a Consolidation Coal company town with many parallels with Mount Savage.

Engines built at Mount Savage for other roads

The following table shows a partial list of construction at Mount Savage for other roads. Narrow gauge equipment was built under contract to T. H. Paul, of Frostburg. Later, Mount Savage began to market their own narrow gauge equipment, built to the Paul pattern. It is probably safe to say that sales after 1883 resulted from the issuance of the catalog.

The Mount Savage Works sent two engines to the National Exposition of Railroad Appliances in Chicago in May of 1883. Both were 3 foot gauge. The 4-4-0 unit had 12"x20" cylinders, 48-inch wheels, and weighed 41,000 pounds. The 2-6-0 unit had 14"x18" cylinders, 40-inch wheels, and weighed 49,000 pounds. The disposition of the engines after the show is unknown.

The catalog listed five basic engine types. Customization of the design could be specified by the customer, for a price. The basic specifications of the various types are given. The first four types are 3-foot narrow gauge, and the fifth is standard gauge. The diameter and stroke of the cylinders, in inches is given, as is the driver wheel diameter. The engine weight in pounds is also listed. It is uncertain what the total production was. The catalog types are:

type	wheel	gauge	cylinders	wheel dia.	weight
1.	0-6-0	36"	9x14	30"	22000
2.	4-4-0	36"	12x18	44"	38000
3.	2-6-0	36"	14x18	40"	49000
4.	2-8-0	36"	15x18	36"	56000
5.	2-8-0	std	20x24	50"	95500

An engine of type 2 went to the East & West Railroad of Alabama. An engine of type 4 went to the Austin & North Western Railroad of Texas. A type 5 engine became West Virginia Central & Pittsburg No. 3.

The production total numbers vary in different sources. White claims 12, Mellander claims 58. The above list includes 24. Total production at Mount Savage is given as 100 units. Mellander claims 42 units went to C & P. The Rehor letter lists nine engines built at Mount Savage for resale by Paul. With the loss of the C & P records at the time of the Western Maryland take-over, the actual production figures may never be known.

1. T. H. Paul, under contract. All are 3' gauge.

    a) Green Ridge Railroad, Allegany County, MD (2 units).

Green Ridge Number 1 (the *Flintstone*, built in 1883) is featured in an illustration of the catalog, as the model for the 0-6-0 units. GRRR Number 2 is an 0-4-0 unit. The rail line was eight miles to the east of Cumberland, in the vicinity of Town Hill, and Fifteen Mile Creek. It belonged to the Mertens family, and supplied lumber to a sawmill at Oldtown, for use by the Merten's boatyards in Cumberland to construct canal boats. The railroad operated from 1889 to 1897. It interchanged with the B&O railroad near Paw Paw, WV, after crossing the Potomac on a trestle. Disposition of the engines is unknown, but they may have gone to the Keystone Coal & Iron Company of Riddlesburg, Pennsylvania.

    b) Pacific Coast RR, Oregon Improvement Co. (3 units)

    no further information is known

    c) Toledo, Delphos & Burlington, Ohio (3 units)

    no additional information is known

    d) Pittsburgh & Western (2 units)

A 2-6-0 unit built in March 1882 as number 3 was not delivered. It was sold in April 1884 to the Bright Hope Railway as their number 3. Disposition is unknown. Another 2-6-0 unit was built as road number 4 in April 1882, and was later sold in November 1887 to the Grafton & Greenbrier railroad as their

No. 4. Disposition is unknown. The Pittsburgh & Western was absorbed into the B&O system in 1902. No Mount Savage engines were listed on the roster at that time.

2. Austin and North Western (A&NW) railroad, Austin, Texas, July 1883.

No. 5, 2-8-0, 3-foot gauge, 15" x 18" cylinders, 28 tons, 36" drivers. This engine was listed as Mount Savage serial No. 33 by the Southern Iron & Equipment (SI&E) Co. in 1918. It went to Tallahalla Lumber Co. It was also listed as SI&E No. 1264, before being sold to the Madrozo Sugar Company of Cuba as their No. 4 on 26 August 1918. It was reported out of service in 1948. Paul also supplied four type 4-4-0 engines to the A&NW. At least two of these may have been built at Mount Savage. The claim to fame of the A&NW is the hauling of 50,000 tons of pink granite for the State Capitol in Austin Texas.

3. Clarksburg, Weston & Midland Railroad.

This engine was purchased new in 1883, and was a 4-4-0 of 36" gauge. The railroad was 3' gauge until 1886. It was a reorganization of the earlier Clarksburg, Weston & Glenville (8/79-4/89). The railroad later became part of the B&O. The engine transitioned to the Lancaster, Oxford & Southern, of Pennsylvania. The LO&S was a reorganization of the earlier Peach Bottom Railway. Engine No. 4 was scrapped in 1916, after a fire.

4. East & West Railroad of Alabama, 4-4-0 engine *John Postall*

The locomotive was built in June of 1883. It featured 12" x 20" cylinders, 48" drivers, and weighed 41,000 pounds. Two more locomotives of the 4-4-0 type, weighing 49,000 pounds, were also delivered at that time. The East & West Railroad was incorporated in 1882, and completed in 1887. It was converted to standard gauge in 1888. the company merged with the Chattahoochee Terminal in 1902 to form the Atlantic & Birmingham Airline Railway. This was acquired by the Seaboard System in 1909. Disposition of the engine is unknown.

5. West Virginia Central & Pittsburgh

1 unit, 2-8-0 numbered 3, later assigned WM number 252. Cylinders 20" x 24", 50" drivers. scrapped 1905. 95,500 pounds, 140 psi, standard gauge. The Claus letter of 1939 (ref. 93) alludes to multiple engines for the West Virginia Central & Pittsburg, which were narrow gauge. No further information on these is known.

6. Allegany Central Railroad, circa 1881, Allegany County, (western) New York state

ACRR No. 3 was a 4-4-0 unit built in Mount Savage in 1882. It had 44 inch drivers, and 12 x 18 cylinders. It was 3 foot gauge. The catalog weight of this model is 38,000 pounds. The engine was named S. C. Dorsey. It was reported scrapped by 1901.

7. Silver City, Deming & Pacific (Territory of New Mexico).

This 3-foot gauge line was opened between Deming, New Mexico and Silver City in 1883, a distance of 47 miles. The line was purchased by the Sante Fe Railroad in Feb. 1884. It was operated for a short while in narrow gauge, then converted to standard gauge. Engine 3 was a Mount Savage product, 2-6-0, built in March 1883, with 40" drivers, and 14" x 18" cylinders. Catalog weight for this unit was 49000 pounds. The disposition of the engine is unknown, but it did not transition to the Santa Fe.

8. Anniston & Atlantic, of Alabama.

This circa 1883 road was started as narrow gauge, in the vicinity of Talladega, completed in 1886. The line was purchased by the Alabama Mineral Railroad in 1889, and converted to 4' 9" gauge. The line was purchased by the Louisville & Nashville. A 4-4-0 engine from Mount Savage, built 1883, was rostered, although it may have come from the Clifton Railroad. The disposition of the engine after removal from service is unknown. There is a picture of this unit in Richard E. Prince's book, Louisville & Nashville Steam Locomotives, p. 21.

9. St. Clairsville Railway, Ohio

This line had about 6.5 miles of 3 foot gauge track. It was operated by the B&O. The name was mentioned in the Claus letter but no further information known.

10. Kemble Coal & Iron

This line was also mentioned in the Claus letter, but no further information known.

11. There are records of a 0-4-0 saddletank locomotive mine locomotive *Artistotle* that may have been built by Paul.

Engines need a tender to carry the coal and water. These were built at Mount Savage as well. The early rule of thumb was that the ratio of water to coal consumption is 7:1. Tenders were constructed from heavy gauge sheet iron, usually 1/8" plate on the sides, and 3/16" on the bottom. Due to rust, these units had approximately a 10-year working life, but were easily repaired. The horseshoe-shape water tank was the favored design. Wooden frames were used until about 1870, when iron frames were substituted. White mentions that the C & P used inside bearing tender trucks. C & P tenders had a water capacity of 5-6000 gallons. Rumor has it that the C & P deliberately used small tenders, because otherwise their engines were "borrowed" by the B&O to do the Brunswick run with loaded coal trains on the weekends. C & P engines left in Cumberland or Piedmont over the weekend were frequently used by the B&O to reduce wear-and-tear on their own motive power fleet.

Railroad infrastructure

Mount Savage Rail Road and the B&O

The Maryland & New York Iron & Coal Co. was charted in 1838, and built several blast furnaces at Mount Savage, Allegany County, Maryland. These furnaces were modeled on the Georges Creek Coal & Iron Company's Lonaconing Furnace. Besides the blast furnaces, facilities were built to work the cast iron, most notably a rolling mill, where the first American made iron rail was manufactured in 1844. Five hundred tons of rail were produced for the company's railroad, following the path of Jennings Run to Will's Creek, and through the Narrows to the B&O railhead at Cumberland. Bridges were originally built of timber, but were later replaced by iron due to excessive maintenance costs.

In February 1844, records indicate that the B&O railroad supplied engines and cars to the Maryland & New York Iron & Coal Company. The 10 mile long Mount Savage Rail Road was completed to Cumberland in 1845, the same year Florida was admitted as a state. The bridge over Will's Creek west of the Narrows towards Mount Savage is dated 1842. The B&O did not send their best equipment into mine service. Engines of the "second class" were used. This classification was based on weight and performance, not quality. To put it in better terms,

"It must be remarked that the duty of the 2nd class engines appears so much less than that of the other classes, not from inferior efficiency, but from circumstances which have given the two engines of this class less to do than they could have accomplished. This is particularly to be said of the engine of this class which has done the work of the Mount Savage Road; this engine being, in fact, one of the best in the service." (21st. Annual Report of the B&O, Oct. 1847, p. 43)

In a week in December 1852, the Mount Savage Rail Road moved more than 5,500 tons of coal to Cumberland. The first commercial contract signed by the

113

Baltimore & Ohio Railroad to move coal was in February 1844 for the Mount Savage product.

April 1, 1845, marked the date of an historic agreement between the B&O Railroad and the Maryland & New York Iron & Coal Co. It stipulated a charge of 1 1/3 cents per ton-mile to transport coal from Cumberland to Baltimore, provided the company shipped at least 175 tons/day for at least 300 days of the year. Coal was still viewed as a speculative commodity by the B&O. Wood or charcoal were the fuel of choice for industry, and for home heating. Connection was made with the B&O in Cumberland in 1846. Also in that year, the B&O contracted for 15 miles of Mount Savage rail, nearly 675 tons of the 51 pounds per yard product then produced. The rail was used to upgrade the line between Harper's Ferry and Baltimore. Before this purchase, the B&O was relying totally on imported British rail.

Ross Winans of Baltimore supplied engines and rolling stock to the Mount Savage Rail Road. It is not known if this is a complete list of Mount Savage motive power. All of the listed engines are of the 0-8-0 'Camel' type. Four of the engines went to the C & P Railroad.

Mount Savage Railroad Motive Power Roster

Builder & P No.	type	date	Name	Company	disposition	C
1. Winans 1891 1	0-8-0	1848	Mount Savage	MSRR	rblt 1868, scrp	
2. Winans n/a	0-8-0	1850	New York	Mount S. Iron	unknown	
3. Winans 1891 2	0-8-0	1852	Highlander	Mount S. Iron	rblt 1868, scrp	
4. Winans scrp 1896 3	0-8-0	1852	Frostburg	Mount S. Iron	rblt 1866, 75.	
5. Winans 1896 4	0-8-0	1853	Galloway Lynn	Mount S. Iron	rblt 1874, scrp	

(John G. Lynn)

114

In 1845, the railroad inaugurated passenger service from Mount Savage, with connections to the B&O in Cumberland. Three trains per day were provided and operated by the B&O. At that time, the trip from Baltimore took 8 1/2 hours. William Cullen Bryant wrote of his trip in the Saturday Evening Post, providing a fascinating glimpse into the rigors of the early travels. He writes, "At Cumberland, you leave the B&O railroad, and enter a single passenger car at the end of a long row of empty coal wagons, which are slowly dragged up a rocky pass beside a shallow stream into the coal regions of the Alleghenies."

The Maryland & New York Iron & Coal Co. failed in 1848, and the assets were sold to the Lulworth Iron Company. The Mount Savage Rail Road was transferred to Lulworth on January 14, 1848. That same year, Lulworth itself reorganized to become the Mount Savage Iron Company. Winans delivered ten coal cars to the company on August 1, 1850, followed by five more in September. He had worked on 6 of the 4-wheel cars previously, in August of 1845. The Mount Savage Iron Company completed the Canal Wharf in Cumberland in 1850.

The Mount Savage Iron Company had extended their rail line northward 3 miles from Mount Savage to Borden Yard in 1851. The main line was double tracked from Cumberland to Mount Savage Junction in 1872, and a third track was added in 1902. Travel west on Route 40 through the Narrows from Cumberland, and the old Western Maryland line, now used by the Western Maryland Scenic RR, will be on your left. The CSX main line across Will's Creek on the right used to be Mount Savage Rail Road, then C & P. The B&O had trackage rights on these lines. The Pennsylvania Railroad came from Bedford near the west end of the Narrows on a bridge, since removed. This would become the Western Maryland State Line Branch, but the PRR once serviced the passenger trade from the original WM station. At the West end of the Narrows, C & P's Eckhart branch split off, and passed under the Western Maryland iron truss bridge, circa 1907.

Mount Savage, operating center of the railroad, is located at milepost 9.4. At Mount Savage were the C & P shops, roundhouse, passenger station, a wye, and the Mount Savage Refractories brickworks. The roundhouse suffered a fire in 1907, and the depot, which resembled the ones in Frostburg and

Lonaconing, was dismantled in 1955. The shop's turntable was not powered, except by strong arms and backs. There were car shops, a freight house and yards, an oil house, machine and pattern shops, and the office building. The Mount Savage town park is located roughly on the site of the roundhouse. The Mount Savage coal ramp was used by the Pioneer Coal Corp., the Cumberland Parker Seam Coal Corp., and the Victory Coal Mines. Five additional companies loaded coal by conveyor (circa 1947). Earlier, the shop's coal tipple serviced local needs. When in full use, the Mount Savage blast furnaces required 150 tons of coal per day.

The C & P Railroad acquired the Mount Savage Rail Road operation in January 1854. This acquisition included the motive power, rolling stock, 14.9 miles of track from Borden to Cumberland, and the Canal Wharf. Thus, the Mount Savage Rail Road disappeared as a separate corporate entity, but became the basis for the next generation of short line railroads of Allegany County, Maryland, and a direct ancestor of present-day CSX Transportation. The critical path through the Cumberland Narrows was built, as we have seen, by the Mount Savage Rail Road. It is still in daily use, as 12,000 horsepower diesel multiple units routinely haul commodities up the Sand Patch grade and through the tunnel, to Pittsburgh, Chicago, and the west.

Cumberland & Pennsylvania Railroad

Facilities

This section covers freight houses, engine houses, and offices. There were ten water tanks located along the C & P main line, with two in Mount Savage.

Water Tanks

Location	mp	gal	dia	height	notes
Mount Savage	9.4	50000	24	16	deep well & steam pump
Shops	9.7	40000	22	16	

The major C & P facilities were in Mount Savage, the heart of the railroad. These included a sand house, an engine house (1888), carpenter shop and supply house, an electrical supply building, a car inspector's office, hose house, and a lumber store. The office building, built in 1902 of locally produced enameled brick, still stands. The brick roundhouse, circa 1907, had a sixty foot deck 'Armstrong' turntable. There was an associated oil house and supply shed. The stone machine shop and car shop from 1866 still survive. The car shop was extended with a wooden structure in 1906.

The blacksmith shop dated from 1900. There was a paint shop, and paint supply house. Next to the two hundred foot long passenger car shed was the tin and upholstery shop. There was also an ash pit and trestle. The power house at the Mount Savage works, circa 1908, included dual 50 kilowatt, 250 volt generators. In addition, there were two large air compressors for the shop tools, a fire pump, a boiler feed pump, and a converted locomotive boiler, 53" in diameter, and 21 feet long.

Mount Savage Roundhouse fire, 1907. The roundhouse suffered extensive damage, but was rebuilt. There was a fire in the car shop in 1939.

The railroad is more than rail and locomotives. The Mount Savage Shops produced other equipment as well.

C & P engines spent as much time running backwards as forwards, so the tenders were typically equipped with lamps and pilots. Two major types of tenders are in evidence. The earlier units have a large box-type oil lamp, and a 'cowcatcher' on the rear. The newer types had an electric lamp, and the cowcatcher is gone. The coal capacity was generally 7-9 tons, and the water capacity was 5-6000 gallons. The engines were always within reach of a source of coal, were usually close to a water supply, and were never far from the home shops.

Not surprisingly, most of the C & P Freight equipment consisted of coal hoppers. The 1923 valuation lists 2,500 freight cars, of which 2,489 are designed to haul coal.

Several types of gondola cars are listed on the roster. Thirteen cars in the number series 616-630 were built by the C & P during 1895-1898, and are of

117

wooden construction. These are listed as 50,000 pounds capacity, and thirty-five feet long.

Maintenance of way (MoW) is necessary for any railroad to maintain the infrastructure, and to respond to accidents and equipment breakdowns. C & P had its own maintenance of way equipment, and, like most railroads, used older equipment pulled from revenue service, and custom rolling stock. The wreck crane, 'Big Hook' number 105 was kept in Mount Savage. This was a 1902 steam unit with steel body and underframe. Besides its use in wreck clean-up, the C & P Big Hook was rented out to assist in heavy lift tasks. After the new windlass for the deep mine at Ocean arrived by flat car, the C & P hook was used to set it into place. The crane was also used to position the road bridge over Wills Creek at Locust Grove, at the West end of the Narrows.

A smaller crane, numbered 102, was constructed by the C & P in 1901, and consisted of a 40,000 capacity wood underframe car equipped with a 5 ton manual crane. It was kept in Franklin. No pictures are known to exist. There were two riggers' flats, No. 103 and 104, 40,000 capacity, built by the C & P in 1904 of wooden construction. These held auxiliary cables and blocks, and sometimes an old tender water tank for the crane. There was also an electric service car, built by C & P in 1889, and numbered 106, based on a 50 foot wooden car. The unique C & P tool car, number 109, was based on a 60,000 lb. capacity wooden car with composite underframe. C & P special car No. 605 was used as a tunnel icebreaker.

There are rumors of a custom snow plow from the Mount Savage shops, but no photos or descriptions have been found. Equipment lists filed with the ICC also show two circa-1898 converted hoppers, numbered 107 & 108, 50,000 lb. capacity, and steel construction. These were typically used for ballast. The ICC roster also lists a cement car, no. 31. This was built by the C & P in 1894, and was a 37 foot wooden unit, with four-wheel arch-bar trucks.

C & P had a valuable asset in the car and locomotive shops in Mount Savage. With the facilities and experience for locomotive and rolling stock rebuilding and repair, C & P was to a great degree self-sufficient. This allowed the recovery of assets that might otherwise have to be abandoned. Even competitors such as the Georges Creek and Cumberland used the shops when necessary, such as the GC&C accident in January 1883 that sent two of its ten locomotives and fifty-one cars off the trestle at Vale Summit. The locomotives were recovered and sent to Mount Savage for repair.

The C & P had two business cars, the first being constructed in the home shops in 1899. Number 15 was 37 feet in length, with a wooden body and underframe, and composite, 4 wheel trucks. Number 101 was purchased from the Pullman Company, and was 75' 6" feet long, with a steel over wooden sheathing body. The frame was metal, and six-wheel trucks with 36" wheels were used. This car was valued at more than $26,000. It was equipped with Westinghouse air brakes, and hot water/steam heat. It had a 60 volt electrical system, using batteries and axle-driven generators. The car had a water supply system, and sported a kitchen, dining room, state rooms, staff quarters, and an observation room. The car was painted Pullman Green, and the interior featured Mexican and Cuban Mahogany. Unfortunately, it would not clear the Frostburg tunnel.

Most of the C & P cabooses were four-wheel units, built at Mount Savage. The 1922 ICC Valuation lists nineteen of these in service, valued at $640. each. They were of wooden construction. The design followed those of the Pennsylvania Railroad and the Western Maryland. Cabooses No. 33 and 34 were 37-foot, wooden bodied, eight wheel units. These were probably older converted passenger coaches. No pictures are known to exist of these units. They were built by the C & P in 1894 and 1898. Early C & P four wheel cabs had cupolas. Following Western Maryland practice, later units did not. No C & P cabooses were involved in the Western Maryland merger in 1953. Four C & P cabs were rostered as Western Maryland Maintenance of Way equipment, including two converted to weed burners. All were scrapped before 1953. Ballast for the line was crushed stone from Kreigbaum, and cinders and granulated slag from Mount Savage.

Locomotive Mount Savage

C & P Railroad Locomotive Number 1 was named *Mount Savage*. This engine was built by Ross Winans of Baltimore. It was a Camel design, wheel arrangement 0-8-0. It had been purchased in 1848 by the Mount Savage Rail Road. It weighed 50,400 pounds, and had 17" x 22" cylinders. Rebuilt at the Mount Savage shops in 1868, it was scrapped in 1891. No pictures of this particular unit are known to exist.

Steamship Mount Savage

The *Mount Savage*, a 452-ton (burden) screw steamship, was built in 1853 at Philadelphia, Pennsylvania. The vessel was sold at auction to Mr. A. C. Hill in 1854 for $10,000. She had cost $40,000 to build. She was renamed *Memphis* in 1857. Chartered by the Navy in September 1858, she served as *USS Memphis* during the Paraguay expedition of late 1858 and early 1859. The steamer was purchased by the Navy in May 1859 and renamed *Mystic* a few weeks later. In June and July 1860, while operating off Africa, she captured two slave ships.

During the first part of the Civil War *Mystic* served in the blockade of the Confederacy's Atlantic Coast. She assisted in the capture or destruction of four blockade runners off North Carolina in June-September 1862, among them the steamers *Emma* and *Sunbeam*. While in the process of taking the latter, on 28 September, she was damaged in collision with USS *State of Georgia*. *Mystic* was employed in the Chesapeake Bay region from late 1862 until the war's end. In May 1863 she supported the Army during an expedition up the York River and in September of that year seized a sailing vessel off Yorktown. USS *Mystic* was sold to private owners in June 1865. Renamed *General Custer*, she disappeared from merchant vessel registers in 1868. Her disposition is unknown.

Opening of the Mount Savage Railroad Extended

Miners' Journal, Cumberland, MD, September 24, 1852

"Monday, the 20th inst. being the day appointed by the Managers of the Mount Savage Iron Company for the opening of the Extension Railroad, connecting the present termination of the Mount Savage Railroad with the mines of the various Coal companies in the neighborhood of Frostburg, everything was most hospitably arranged for the reception and accommodation of the various guests invited from the vicinity; and a large and happy party of ladies and gentlemen assembled in Cumberland, and entered the cars prepared for them.

It may not be amiss here to give our readers a short description of the Mount Savage Railroad, now the principal feeder of the Baltimore and Ohio Railroad and the Chesapeake and Ohio Canal, with the renowned semi-bituminous coal of this region. It leaves Cumberland, where it unites with the Canal and Baltimore Railroad by separate branches, passing within an easy grade through the sublime scenery of the Narrows of Wills' Mountain, which is crested with a granular white stone of pure silex, destined, at no distant day, to add to the wealth and population of Cumberland in the manufacture of every kind of glass, for which it is admirably calculated.

At the western entrance to the gorge, two miles from Cumberland, the Railroad is intersected by one leading up the valley of Braddock's Run, to the Eckhart, Washington, Pompey Smash, and other valuable Mines. This Road, built by the Maryland Mining Company, as we; as the greater part of the coal property just mentioned, is now owned by the Cumberland Coal and Iron Company.

From this point, the Mount Savage Road proceeds two miles up Wills Creek, crossing that stream by a handsome timber bridge of two arches, each being eighty-five feet span. The gradual decay of timber requiring constant repair, the Company have it in contemplation to erect, in its place, an elegant and substantial iron bridge.

On reaching the mouth of Jennon's (sic) Run, the heavy grade of one hundred feet to the mile commences; and in three miles, at the elevation of nine hundred and eighty feet above tide water, this iron artery first enters the Coal field, to draw from thence the life of a thousand gigantic ocean steamers, ploughing their unvarying, rapid course, in spite of wind and tide, to every known quarter of the world.

The first mines reached are those of the Parker Vein Coal Company, at Barrellville, on the north fork of Jennon's (sic) Run, under the management of M. P. O'Hern, Esq. A Railroad, three quarters of a mile in length, and spanning Jennon's (sic) Run by an elegant Viaduct forty feet in height and three hundred in length, connects them with the main Road, while their little mining village, with its clean and pretty cottages, presents a picturesque appearance. The Parker Vein was the first discovered and earliest mined in the Coal field, and was boated down the Potomac for use in the Government Arsenal at Harper's Ferry, long before the iron age of Railroads had commenced.

Two miles further brings us to Mount Savage-the largest Iron Works in the United States.

Three immense furnaces, which, when in blast, can produce fifteen thousand tons of pig iron a year-a large and most complete foundry and machine shop-a noble rolling mill, capable of turning out ten thousand tons of rails or bar iron a year, or even more-a manufactory of the best fire brick in the United States-dwellings for twelve hundred operatives and their families, estimated at a population of fully five thousand-all this bursts on the view as we arrive at the beautifully situated village of Mount Savage. But now, from the want of protection to the Iron interests of this country, and the low rate of wages abroad, the dwellings are deserted, and the silent furnaces and rolling mill serve only to show how much injury has been effected by this most unwise policy. It is hoped, however, that the recent rise in iron will again put these works in operation, which would prove an immense boon to the working population in the neighborhood.

Here commences the continuation of the Railroad.

It has been extended to five miles in length, so as to overcome the elevation by a grade not exceeding one hundred and five feet to the mile. Some of the embankments are very heavy; the whole road is of a most substantial character, thoroughly ballasted, and laid with Winslow's Patent heavy compound Rail of 65 pounds to the yard. It is needless to add that the Rails were made at Mount Savage. The road reflects the highest credit on C.F. Fogg, the Engineer, to whom was entrusted the entire management.

The first mines passed are those of the Alleghany Company, E. K. Huntley, Esq., Superintendent; and one mile further, at the foot of Frostburg Hill, are the Depots of the Frostburg Coal Company, under the superintendence of D. C. Bruce, Esq., and the Borden Company, under that of A. C. Greene, Esq. Besides the Coal companies already at work, are many others-the Wilthers, the New York, Cumberland Coal and Iron Company, &c.-all possessing large and valuable coal mines, which, at a future day, will tend to swell the amount of transportation on this Railroad. The Cumberland Coal and Iron Company have a large and valuable portion of their coal property coming out on this valley at this point, connecting with their larger deposits on George's Creek; and it is contemplated by the Mount Savage Company, at no distant day, to construct a locomotive tunnel through the big vein under Frostburg Hill, to the valley of George's Creek- a comparatively short distance; which would open a market to an immense area of coal field, so as to bring, by this route, the mineral deposits extending to Lonaconing, which would otherwise have no other outlet than the Railroad down George's Creek, through Westernport, and then over twenty-seven miles of the Baltimore and Ohio Railroad to Cumberland.

The present weekly transportation of Coal, down the Mount Savage Railroad, is nearly six thousand tons; and the greatly increased facilities afforded by the opening of this new line, will, in the course of the next few weeks, increase it to nearly ten thousand.

On the brow of the hill, overlooking the Railroad and depots, is the elegant Italian villa now building for A. C. Greene, Esq., and to this the company adjourned, to partake of a collation and champagne, generously provided for them by the Mount Savage Company.

The company then reentered the cars, and rapidly descending the grade, returned to Cumberland, highly gratified with their excursion."

In Conclusion...

Where many hundreds of men labored in literally hellish conditions, a stranglehold on the rail industry by British industry was broken, and the tools for enabling the industrial expansion of the United States were produced. Much of the work of the First Industrial Revolution took place in Western Maryland. The area missed the steel production facilities that were built in Pittsburgh, but maybe that's a good thing. Western Maryland still benefited by supplying raw material, coal and fireclay. There's only a few artifacts of all this effort left – the shells of the iron furnaces at Lonaconing and Mount Savage. The rail lines are still in use, and the area is honeycombed underground by hundreds of cola mines. But the production of goods migrated elsewhere, and with that went the manufacturing jobs. Western Maryland is a microcosm of the Industrial Revolutions in America.

Glossary of iron making terms

Bessemer Converter – furnace to make steel from iron by removing contaminants.

Bituminous coal – an organic sedimentary rock of mostly carbon.

Blacksmith – creates items from wrought iron.

Blast furnace – furnace to produce iron from iron, and using a forced blast of air to get better combustion.

Bloom – a porous mass of iron and slag, called sponge iron.

Bloomery – a crude iron production facility for small batches.

Blowing engine – a large cylinder powered by a steam engine to produce the blast for the furnace.

Bog iron – poor quality iron made from ore found in swampy areas.

Bosh - lower part of a blast furnace, between the hearth and the stack.

Chafery – a reheating hearth, to work pig iron into wrought iron.

Charcoal – produced by heating wood in the absence of oxygen. Nearly pure carbon.

Coal – a mineral, mostly carbon, with a variety of other trace elements.

Coal gas – by product of coke production

Coke – produced by destructive distillation of coal. Is mostly pure carbon.

Finery forge – facility to produce wrought iron from pig iron, by removing carbon.

Fire clay – silica and alumina.

Flux – material to bind with and capture the impurities in the iron ore.

Forge – a heating furnace with forced draft, fueled by charcoal or coal.

Hematite – iron ore, predominate in Western Maryland

Iron - element number 26.

Limestone – sedimentary rock, calcium carbonate.

Open Hearth Furnace – converts pig iron to steel. Replacement for the Bessemer furnace.

Puddlers candle – bubbles of carbon monoxide produced in a puddling furnace. Burst at catch fire at the surface.

Pig iron – iron ore with the oxygen removed. Iron ore is rust – iron bonded with Oxygen.

Puddling furnace – converts pig iron to steel or wrought iron. Hot air passes over the molten iron.

Reducing agent – removes oxygen from a material. Carbon is used with iron.
Reduction process – opposite of oxidation. Oxygen is removed.
Reverberatory furnace – used to make iron and mild steel. The molten iron is isolated from contact with the fuel, but does contact the combustion gases.
Rolling Mill – process to shape hot iron into long sheets by squeezing between rollers.
Siemens regenerative furnace – circa 1865 open hearth furnace design.
Slag – the impurities extracted from the iron ore; a glassy material when cooled.
Smelting - extractive technique in metallurgy to produce metal from ore.
Steel – iron with a carbon percentage of 0.2 to 2.14%. Stronger than iron.
Tuyeres – nozzle to introduce the blast into the furnace. Water-cooled.
Wrought iron – pig iron worked to reduce contaminants and carbon.

Bibliography

Alderton, Jeff "Time Capsule, Silk Mill on first statewide list of threatened historic properties," Cumberland Times-News, March 28, 2007.

Aldridge, Howard Redford. "The Mount Savage Iron Works," 1924, Record of Phi Mu Fraternity, University of Maryland at College Park Libraries. Special thanks to Mrs. H. Aldridge, Frostburg, Maryland for a copy of her husband's paper on the Mount Savage Iron Works. Also see J. Alleghenies, Vol. XIV-1978.

Alexander, John H. "George's Creek Coal and Iron Company," 1836. [Baltimore?, 1837], available: Frostburg State University Library: Special Collections, Call No. : TN805.Z6G3. also Pratt Library, D9549.G4A3q.

Allen, Jay Douglas. "The Mount Savage Iron Works, Mount Savage, Maryland a case study in pre-Civil War industrial development," 1970, Thesis (M.A.) - University of Maryland.

Beachley, Charles E. *History of the Consolidated Coal Company* 1864-1934, 1934, Consolidation Coal Company, New York.

Best, G. M. "Thomas H. Paul & Son, Locomotive Builders," Locomotive & Railroad Historical Society (L&RHS) Bulletin 141, Autumn, 1979, pp. 19-26.

Bishop, James W. *The Glass Industry of Allegany County, Maryland,* 1968, Commercial Press Printing, Cumberland, Maryland.

Blevins, Danny K. *Van Lear (KY)* Feb 2008, Arcadia Publishing, Images of America Series, ISBN 0738552941.

Bowen, Ele [sic]. *Rambles in the Path of the Steam-Horse,.* Philadelphia: William Bromwell and William White, 1855.

Bowen, Mary "Mount Savage, Allegany County, Maryland" presented to the Homemakers Club of Mount Savage 1953.

Bryant, William Cullen, "Mount Savage, 1860," Saturday Evening Post, 1860, Reprinted in Tableland Trails, Vol. I, No. 3, Fall, 1953, Oakland, Maryland.

Buckley, Geoffrey L. *Extracting Appalachia: Images of Consolidation Coal Company*, 2004, Ohio University Press, ISBN 0821415557.

Carney, Charles, "The History of Mount Savage," May 1967, Project 67-014-005, Cooperative Extensive Service, University of Maryland.

Clark, William Bullock *Maryland Geological Survey, Allegany County*, 1900, Johns Hopkins Press, Baltimore, Maryland.

Clark, William Bullock *Maryland Geological Survey: The Limestones of Maryland*. Special publication of VIII, Part III, JHU Press, 1910, (avail. ASIN: B005HZKQLQ)

Davis, Dr. Feather Ann, *The Rise and Fall of the Industrial Revolution Along the Gwinns Falls* Baltimore county, Maryland. http://www.dickeyville.org/images/rise&fall.pdf

Deffenbaugh, Mrs. Roy, "History of Mount Savage, Maryland," 1968, Mount Savage High School.

Dilts, James D. *The Great Road The Building of the Baltimore and Ohio The Nation's First Railroad, 1828-1853*, 1993, Stanford University Press.

Francis, C. B. *The Making, Shaping and Treatment of Steel* 5th ed. United States Steel, 1940, Carnegie-Illinois Steel Corp.

Feldstein, Albert L. *Feldstein's Historic Coal Mining and Railroads of Allegany County, Maryland*, Publisher: Albert L. Feldstein, 2000, ISBN 0-9701605-0-X.

Gordon, Robert B. *American Iron 1607-1900*, JHU Press, ISBN-0801868165, 2001.

Harvey, Katherine A. *The Best-Dressed Miners - Life and Labor in the Maryland Coal Region 1835-1910*, 1969, Cornell University Press.

Harvey, Katherine A. "The Lonaconing Journals: The Founding of a Coal and Iron Community 1837-1840," March 1977, Transactions of the American Philosophical Society, Philadelphia, Vol. 67, Part 2.

Hicks, W. Ray, "The Georges Creek and Cumberland Railroad," March, 1952, Locomotive & Railway Historical Society Bulletin, No. 85.

Hindle, Brooke; Lubar, Steven Engines of Change, The American Industrial Revolution 1790-1860, 1986, Smithsonian Institution.

Hughes, George Wurtz, "Extracts from reports of an examination of the coal measures belonging to the Maryland mining company, in Allegany county; and of a survey for railroad from the mines to the Chesapeake and Ohio canal, at Cumberland," 1837, Printed by Gales and Seaton, Washington (available: Pratt Library, Baltimore).

Hunt J. William, "CUMBERLAND & PENNSYLVANIA Make Tracks in Early Years," April 25, 1965, Cumberland Times, *Across the Desk*.

Lacoste, Kenneth C., Wall, Robert D. *An Archeological Study of the Western Maryland Coal Region: The Historic Resources*, 1989, Maryland Geological Survey.

Lee, Albin, "The Austin & Northwestern Railroad," Jan./Feb. 1990, Narrow Gauge and Short Line Gazette , pp. 60-63. (T. H. Paul).

Lesley, J. Peter. *The Iron Manufacturer's Guide to the Furnaces, Forges, and Rolling Mills of the United States,*. New York: John Wiley, 1859.

Mellander, Deane. *Rails to the Big Vein, the Short Lines of Allegany County, Maryland*, January, 1981, Potomac Chapter, NRHS, Inc.

Mellander, Deane. *Cumberland and Pennsylvania Railroad*, 1981, Carstens Publishers, Inc., ISBN 911868-42-9.

Minor, D.K. (ed.), American Railroad Journal, Summer, 1844, tour of Mount Savage.

Nicolls, William Japser. *Above Ground and Below in the Georges Creek Coal Region,* 1898, Consolidation Coal Company, Baltimore.

Otto, Mary "Grasping for a Thread of Hope, Long-Shut Silk Mill's Memories Inspire Preservation Effort", Washington Post, September 7, 2004; Page B01.

Paul, Amanda *Mount Savage, Images of America Series*, Arcadia Publishing, August 25, 2004, ISBN- 0738516805.

Pearson, Henry *An American Railroad Builder: John Murray Forbes*, Houghton, Mifflin & Co., 1911.

Poor, H.V. and H.W., *Poor's Manual of Railroads*, 1884," 1884, 17th Annual Number, and others.

Randolph, B.S. "History of the Maryland Coal Region," Journal of the Alleghenies, Vol. XXIX-1993, pp. 47-62.

Rankin, Robert G., "Report on Cumberland Coal Basin," 1855, New York: John F. Trow, Printer

Richards, William M. "An Experiment in Industrial Feudalism at Lonaconing, Maryland 1837-1860." M.A. Thesis, University of Maryland, 1950.

Scharf, J. Thomas, *History of Western Maryland, being a history of Frederick, Montgomery, Carroll, Washington, Allegany, and Garrett Counties from the earliest period to the present day, including biographical sketches of their representative men*, 2 volumes, Philadelphia, 1882.

Schwartz, Lee G.; Feldstein, Albert; Baldwin, Joan H. *Allegany County, A Pictorial History*, 1980, The Donning Co., Virginia Beach, Virginia.

Singewald, Jr., Joseph T. *Report on the Iron Ores of Maryland, with an Account of the Iron Industry*, Part III of Maryland Geologic Survey, volume nine, Baltimore: JHU Press, 1911.

Smith, Gene Lee & Grant, 1984, Promontory Press, pp 358-360 (re: T. H. Paul locomotive).

Stakem, Patrick H. *Cumberland & Pennsylvania Railroad Revisited*, 2002, Pats Railroad Books. ISBN 0-9725966-0-7.

Stakem, Patrick H., "The Georges Creek Railroad 1853-1863," Nov. 1995, The Automatic Block, Vol. 17, No. 11. The Automatic Block is the newsletter of the Western Maryland Chapter of the National Railway Historical Society in Cumberland, Maryland.

Stakem, Patrick H., "Coal to the Western Terminus; Canal-Railroad Connections in Cumberland, Maryland" Sept. 1995, On the Towpath, publication of the C&O Canal Historical Society, Vol. XXVII, no. 3, p. 10-11.

Stakem, Patrick H. "The Earliest Railroad Activities in Western Maryland, 1828-1870," 1996, J. Alleghenies, Vol. XXXII, ISSN-0276-7449.

Stakem, Patrick H., "The Mount Savage Rail Road 1845-1854,"June 1995, The Automatic Block, Vol. 17, No. 6; reprinted in Cumberland Times, Sept. 30, 1995, Railfest special section.

Stakem, Patrick H., "T.H. Paul & Sons, Locomotive Builders, Frostburg, Maryland 1855-1883," Jan. 1992, The Automatic Block, Vol. 14, No. 1.

Stakem, Patrick H. "The Mount Savage Locomotive Shops," National Railway Historical Society (NRHS) Bulletin, Spring/Summer 1997.

Stakem, Patrick H. "T.H. Paul, Master Locomotive Builder of Frostburg, Journal of the Alleghenies, 1997.

Stakem, Patrick H. and Stakem, Patrick E. *From the (Iron) Horses Mouth An updated Roster from Ross Winans' Memorandum of Engines*, 2008, ISBN 0-9725966-2-3, Oct. 2008, Pats Railroad Books.

Stakem, Patrick H., "Engine #5," 1995, March, 1996, The Automatic Block, Vol. 18 no. 3. (T. H. Paul).

Strapac, Joseph A. *Cotton Belt Locomotives,* Oct. 99, Indiana University Press. (T.H. Paul).

Stegmaier, Harry, Jr., et al. *Allegany County - A History*, 1976, McClain Publishing, Parsons, West Virginia.

Thomas, LL.D., James W., Williams, Judge T.J.C. *History of Allegany County, Maryland,* 1923, reprinted 1969, Baltimore, Regional Publishing Co. (p. 626-628, Millholland).

Urbas, Anton "Georges Creek & Cumberland Railroad Passenger Train Service," 1993, J. Alleghenies, Vol. XXIX-1993, pp. 38-47.

Walsh & Fox. *Maryland: A History: 1632 - 1974*, Maryland Historical Society, Baltimore, 1974.

Ware, Donna M., *Green Glades and Sooty Gob Piles*, 1991, Maryland Historical Trust.

Weld, Henry Thomas "A Report made by Henry Thomas Weld, esq., of the Maryland and New York Iron and Coal Company's lands in the county of Alleghany (sic) and State of Maryland. 1839. Lehigh University Library, Bethlehem, Pennsylvania.

White, John H. "James Millholland and Early Railroad Engineering". Contributions From the Museum of History and Technology #252 (1968): 3-36.

White, John H. Jr. *A History of the American Locomotive Its Development 1830-1880*, 1968, Dover Publications, Reprinted 1979, ISBN 0-486-23818-0.

White, John H. Jr. *Early American Locomotives*, 1972, Dover Publications, ISBN 0-486-22772-3.

White, John H. *A Short History of American Locomotive Building in the Steam Era,* Bass Books, 1982, Washington, D.C.

Wigginton, Eliot (ed), Foxfire 5, 1979, Anchor Books, p. 77-207. (Iron manufacturing).

Wyckoff, William C. *Silk Manufacturing in the United States,* 1883, Silk Association of America.

Resources

Dictionary of American Biography, 1930, New York: Charles Scribner's Sons.

"Lonaconing - Home in the Hills," 1986, Lonaconing, Maryland.

Report of President & Board of Directors of Cumberland Coal & Iron Company to the Stockholders, Feb. 11, 1853, New York: John F. Trow, Printer.

James A. Millholland Collection, 1866-1899 #163, Archives Center, National Museum of American History, Smithsonian Institution.

Allegany High School (Cumberland, MD) Oral History Project.

Society of Industrial Archeology, Vol. 36 No 3 Summer 2007 (Silk Mill).

www.cumberlandglass.org

J. Alleghenies, Vol. XXII, 1986, on the Silk Mill

"92 Years of Transportation Progress by the CUMBERLAND & PENNSYLVANIA Railroad and its Contribution towards the Development of Cumberland, and Allegany County, Maryland," 1937, CUMBERLAND & PENNSYLVANIA Railroad, Cumberland, Maryland

Charters, Acts of Legislation, and By-laws relating to the Consolidation Coal Company and the Cumberland and Pennsylvania Railroad Company of Maryland, 1872, New York, William R. Vidal, Stationer.

Cumberland & Pennsylvania Railroad Company Wage Schedule, 1918, ahthor's collection.

Cumberland Sunday Times, March 24, 1957. (Mt. Savage)

Frostburg Mining Journal, Jan. 13, 1872 (passenger service).

Interstate Commerce Commission Valuation Report on the C & P RR, 1923, residing in the National Archives II Facility, College Park, Maryland

Rail Tracks in Allegany County, Maryland, Book 1, 1980, Preservation Society of Allegany County, Maryland, Cumberland, Maryland.

Heritage Review, newsletter of the Preservation Society of Allegany County, Cumberland, Maryland. Various issues. Vol. 27, No. 10, Oct. 1999 has an article on the iron mines.

"Manufacture of Railway Iron in Mount Savage"Scientific American, Vol. 6, No.   8 November 9, 1850.

New York Times, March 31, 1858, Page 2, regarding beginning operations of the rolling mill at Mount Savage.

Harper's Monthly, April 1, 1857, June Jaunt, by Brantz Mayer. (Mount Savage)

New York Times, Dec. 13, 1852, "During the week ending the 4th inst , 5.514 tons of coal were transported over the Mount Savage Railroad, 3999 tons over the Cumberland Coal and Iron... "

Washington Post, Sept 4, 1897 "The Lulworth tennis tourney, at Mount Savage, a notable society event, which continued three days, ended with the following as champions for 1897...".

Scientific American, Vol. 3, No. 9, Nov 20, 1847, "The Mount Savage Iron Works have been sold by the Sheriff for over $200000. The purchasers were Messrs. Corning and Winslow of Albany, N. Y. "

Scientific American, Sept. 11, 1847, Vol. 2, No. 51, "The Mount Savage Iron Works are to be sold on the 9th of October, under execution, at the suit of the English bond holders and others...."

http://www.history.navy.mil/photos/sh-civil/civsh-m/mt-savge.htm
Steamship Mount Savage

www.mountsavagehistoricalsociety.org

"Opening of the Mount Savage Railroad Extended," Miners Journal, Cumberland, MD Sept 24, 1852.

Allegany County Deed, Mount Savage Iron to C & P RR, Jan 2, 1854, Ref: 12-339, author's collection.

J. Franklin Institute, Vol. 38, Dec. 1844, pp 382-283, award #2705.

Mount Savage Maryland in the News, Vol. 1 & 2, 2010, Mount Savage Historical society, Mount Savage, Maryland.

Frostburg City Directory, Ort Library, Frostburg University.

J. Alleghenies, Vol. XXIX-1993, p. 80. (T. H. Paul).

Frostburg Mining Journal, (Microfilm, Frostburg University Ort Library) (T.H. Paul

- late 1880, re: 2-6-0 engine for Kansas & Gulf
- b) June 1882, re: engines to Oregon
- c) March 15, 1890 re: 4 hp gas engine
- d) May 24, 1890 re: to Sioux City, Iowa
- e) April 27, 1872
- also, Cumberland Civilian, August 19, 1883, re: receivership.

Letter of Feb. 18, 1963, Rehor to Fisher, subject: Feb. 10, 1883 Baltimore Manufacturers Records, and reprint of Railroad Gazette of Feb. 16, 1883 (article on T.H. Paul).

Letter from Mr. Claus, General Manager of C & P to Mr. Charles E. Fisher, L&RHS, dated March 23, 1939, Cumberland, MD, concerning Mt. Savage production.

(Note: these letters have disappeared from the archives of the L&RHS; apparently, Mr. Rehor directed that his correspondence be disposed of at his death.)

US Patent 470629, 1892 "Apparatus for Making Illuminating Gas." also Patent 530237, 1894, "Gas Engine" (T. H. Paul).

Patents

The following patents relate to Lonaconing and Mount Savage activities. The full text of patents can be found at the Patent Office website, and on Google patents.

• *Improvement in the Construction and Heating of Furnaces for Metallurgic Operations*, C.E. Detmold of New York, N.Y. Number 3,176, July 1843.

• *Method of Effecting Combustion in Furnaces and Flues of Steam Boilers*, C. E. Detmold, NY, 1843, Number 33645A

• *Mode of Securing the Ends of Railway Bars*, C.E. Detmold, 22,168, Nov. 1858.

• *Rolling Railway-Bars*, John W. Brown, Savage Iron Works, Allegany County, Maryland, 14552, April 1856.

• *Improved Machine for Compressing Puddle-balls*, John F. Winslow, 34177, 1862.

• *Malleable Iron from Ores*, John F. Winslow, 4526, 1846, Troy, NY.

• *Rolling Puddlers Bars into Blooms*, John F. Winslow, Troy, N.Y., Number 5660, July 1848.

Appendix – The J. W. Brown Rolling Mill Patent

UNITED STATES PATENT OFFICE.

JOHN W. BROWN, OF SAVAGE IRON WORKS, ALLEGANY COUNTY, MARYLAND.

ROLLING RAILWAY-BARS.

Specification of Letters Patent No. 14,552, dated April 1, 1856.

To all whom it may concern:

Be it known that I, JOHN W. BROWN, of Mount Savage Iron Works, in the county of Allegany and State of Maryland, have invented a new and useful Improvement in Machinery for Rolling T-Iron Rails for Railroad and other Uses; and I do hereby declare that the following is a full, clear, and exact description of the same, reference being had to the accompanying drawings, forming part of this specification, in which—

Figure 1, is a front elevation of a rolling mill for carrying out my invention. Fig. 2, is a diagram representing sections of the groove 4, and illustrating the operation of my improvement. Fig. 3, is a diagram illustrating the change of form which the bar undergoes in passing through the groove, 3, of the roller.

Similar letters of reference indicate corresponding parts in the several figures.

This improvement has for its object the rolling of the bars into such forms successively, as to cause all parts of the rail to be submitted in the rolling process to as nearly as possible a uniform degree of drawing and compression, thereby preventing the separation of the head and flange, or any part being drawn sufficiently to break the other parts in pieces, and making all parts of the rail of equal density. The improvement enables rails to be made perfectly sound with crystalline iron in the heads, which is far superior to fibrous iron, as the latter laminates or peels off.

In the rollers, A, B, of the rolling mill represented, are five grooves, numbered respectively in Fig. 1, from 1 to 5, in the order of succession in which they receive the bar to roll it, the bar being taken from the roughing or billeting rollers and passed through groove, 1, and afterward through 2, 3, 4 and 5, the latter of which finishes it.

The improvement consists in the form of the groove, 3, by which a depression or cavity is formed all along the center of the base of the rail, after the reduction to form the head has been to a certain extent effected by the grooves 1 and 2, but before the further reduction to form the neck is commenced; so that by the subsequent operation of the groove, 4, which reduces the middle of the bar to form the neck, and brings it nearly to the proper shape, the metal is easily displaced from the middle of the bar and driven toward the base, to fill the depression or cavity which has been made by the upper roller, A, in the middle of the base, during the passage of the bar through the groove, 3.

To show the direction in which the metal is displaced from the center of the bar toward the base, the diagram, Fig. 3, represents the two forms of the bar after leaving the groove, 3, and after leaving the groove, 4, the former being shown in black outline and the latter in red; the depression or cavity in the base produced in the groove, 3, being indicated by the letter, *a*. The effect which the previous formation of the depression or cavity, *a*, has in the rolling of the bar in the groove, 4, is illustrated in Fig. 2, where the three pairs of circles, *b*, *c*, *d*, represent severally those parts of the groove, 4, of the roller which respectively roll the flanges of the base, the neck, and the head. C, in the same figure, represents that portion of the bar which has not yet entered the groove, 4; and D, that portion which has passed through the said groove; the lines, *e*, *e*, represent the base of the rail; those *f*, *f*, the head; and the dotted lines, *g*, *g*, the neck. In this figure it is shown that the largest parts, *d*, *d*, of the rollers come into action on the bar as the latter arrives at the position of the red line, *h*, but the parts, *b*, *b*, do not come into operation till the bar arrives at the position of the red line, *i*, and the parts, *c*, *c*, not till the bar has reached the position of the red line, *j*, by which means the iron is forced by the parts, *d*, *d*, from the middle of the bar toward the collar, *k*, of the roller, B, against which the base of the rail is formed, (see Fig. 2), before any of the parts that roll the head and flanges come into action. The middle of the bar is in this way reduced to two-thirds of the thickness it was at the time of entering the rollers, before the flanges are operated upon, and by the time the operation on the head of the rail commences, it is reduced nearly to the proper thickness for the neck of the rail, and the depression or cavity in the base is quite filled up, and the several parts of the rollers being properly proportioned, there will be no more thickness left in the middle of the bar to extend it lengthwise than there is in the base and head; and consequently all parts of the rail will be drawn or extended lengthwise in a like degree and be

of equal density. Those of the grooves of
the rollers which are not particularly described, are assumed to be similar to those
in the rollers of other rolling mills for the
5 same purpose.

What I claim as my invention, and de-
sire to secure by Letters Patent, is—

So forming one or more of the grooves
of the rollers, as shown substantially at 3,
10 Fig. 1, as to produce a depression or cavity
all along that side of the bar which is to
form the base of the rail, previously to
the reduction of the bar to form the neck;
said cavity to be filled up by the displacement of the iron from the middle of the 15
rail by the subsequent rolling operation,
substantially as set forth for the purpose
herein described.

JOHN W. BROWN.

Witnesses:
   SAMUEL DANKS,
   JAMES WHITEHEAD.

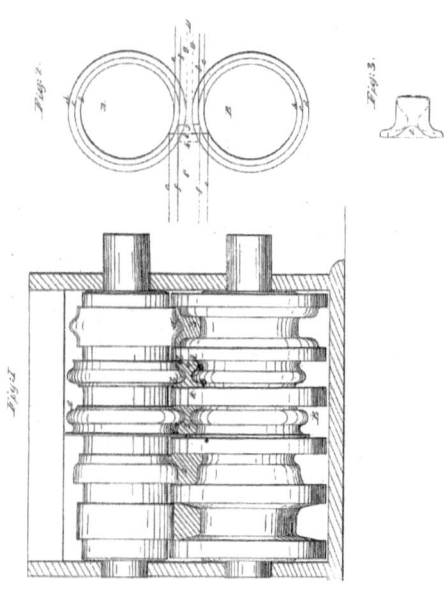

J. W. Brown,

Rolling Railroad Rails,

Nº14,552.   Patented Apr. 1, 1856.

If you enjoyed this book, you might enjoy some of the author's other titles.

Stakem, Patrick H. *The History of the Industrial Revolution in Western Maryland,* 2011, PRRB Publishing, ASIN B004LX0JB2.

Stakem, Patrick H. *Cumberland & Pennsylvania Railroad Revisited*, 2011, PRRB Publishing, ASIN B004J8HUAM.

Stakem, Patrick H. *Eckhart Mines, The National Road, and the Eckhart Railroad*, 2011, PRRB Publishing, ASIN B004KSQVWO.

Stakem, Patrick H. *Down the 'crick: the Georges Creek Valley of Western Maryland,* 2014, PRRB Publishing, ASIN B00LDT94UY.

Stakem, Patrick H. *Lonaconing Residency, Iron Technology & the Railroad,* 2011, PRRB Publishing, ASIN B004L62DNQ..

Stakem, Patrick H. *T. H. Paul & J. A. Millhollland: Master Locomotive Builders of Western Maryland*, 2011, PRRB Publishing, ASIN B004LGT00U.

Stakem, Patrick H. *Tracks along the Ditch, Relationships between the C&O Canal and the Railroads*, 2012, PRRB Publishing, ASIN B008LB6VKI.

Stakem, Patrick H. *From the Iron Horse's Mouth: an Updated Roster from Ross Winans' Memorandum of Engines*, 2011, PRRB Publishing, ASIN B005GM4012.

Stakem, Patrick H. *Iron Manufacturing in 19th Century Western Maryland,* 2015, PRRB Publishing, ASIN B00SNM5EIU.

Stakem, Patrick H. *Railroading around Cumberland*, 2012, Arcadia Press, ISBN- 0738553654.

Stakem, Patrick H. *Cumberland (Then and Now)*, 2012 , Arcadia Press, ISBN- 0738586986 , ASIN B009460QNM

www.ingramcontent.com/pod-product-compliance
Lightning Source LLC
Chambersburg PA
CBHW050452290526
45786CB00006B/2256